Principles

How to Create a

Principled Business Culture

Sid Mickle

This book is dedicated to the wonderful people I had the privilege of knowing and working with at Outer Circle Products in Chicago, IL. Our time together at 860 West Evergreen Street, even on the worst of days, were the very best days of my career.

I may not know exactly what I am doing, and I might do a lot of things poorly, but you can be sure I will try my best every day. I will never lie to you, and I will never disrespect your opinion. I hope we are all successful and I hope we have one hell of a good time together. – An excerpt from a note by the author to his first sales team in the Memphis District, August, 1987.

This is a Review of The Outer Circle Products

Business Environment

Principles

How to Create a

Principled Business Culture

Other books by Sid Mickle Include:

A Backwards Glance

This book is a collection of memories of a southern childhood and beyond.

A Backwards Glance is a retelling of stories from the extraordinary life of an exceptional man. This book follows Sid Mickle from his small-town Alabama childhood to a 40-year professional career that allowed him to travel far from home without ever forgetting its lessons. The story is much more than a memoir, it is a reflection and examination of a life with wonderful friends, family and events. There is success and failure, joy and tragedy, setbacks and triumphs.

These stories include vivid recollections of childhood struggles to understand his polar-opposite parents, race relations, the culture and politics of the era of Vietnam and civil rights. They also feature reflections of a far-flung professional career filled with highs and lows, and a journey that eventually brought the author back to his beginnings. These stories read like fiction, but the events and characters are entirely real.

This story, How to Create a Principles Business Culture, began as a telling of a brief period of the author's life at a new and great company in Chicago. It developed into a self-reflection and review of important events in his life. The writing of this book began fifteen years ago and hopefully provides readers with similar illustrations of good and tough times from living a full life.

Who Killed Glenna?

A murder mystery novel about a tragic death in a small southern town and the first offering in the Sam Bennett series.

Glenna McMann had been shunned, teased, and bullied since the seventh grade. Her rural Alabama classmates, especially the boys, enjoyed making nasty comments about the early development of her body, especially her breasts. She dealt with painful social pressures all alone because she was from an uneducated and uncaring family. Her life was tortured and lonely. Sam Bennett is a local high school football star who protects her during a physical attack, which leads to a brief encounter. His protecting her from Bobby and Tommy Jackson creates a deep hatred by the brothers, and leads them to plot against Sam and Glenna. When she is brutally murdered, the question to her classmates, parents, townspeople and Sam becomes, "Who really killed Glenna McMann"?

Sam and his best friend, Nolan, earn scholarships, fulfilling their dreams of being college athletes. Sam's misunderstood connection to Glenna and Bobby Jackson's plotting make him a murder suspect and he loses his scholarship while Nolan becomes a rising star. Sam joins the Army and serves in the bloody, vicious Vietnam conflict. Before Vietnam, he thought he had experienced terrible things, but the war is a horror beyond his imagination. The twist to the story is who else dies in this coming-of-age story of hatred, betrayal, pain and recovery.

If you like southern fiction, you should enjoy, "Who Killed Glenna?"

A Few Bad Men

The second thriller from the Sam Bennett series.

"A Few Bad Men" begins with a reunion of Vietnam veterans who served together and experienced the horrors of a war fought without a plan to win. They overcome their physical and mental wounds to join together in a fight to stop members of a well-financed Chinese drug ring known as "The Big Circle Boys". This drug cartel are partners with rogue US Army Colonel, Vernon Delano, directing the flow of heroin into Sam's rural Alabama county as a primary stateside distribution point.

Small town political corruption, intimidation and terror rule until Sam's team begins to fight a new war. Death and destruction intrude into the daily lives of small-town folks while they fight to stop the evil people in powerful positions around them.

Lives are lost, and families are destroyed in the fight against influential businessmen and corrupt politicians who turn their backs on everyone. A hunger for power, influence and huge amounts of money are revealed in, "A Few Bad Men".

The Expected Publish Date for "A Few Bad Men" is Fall 2021.

If I Could Turn Back Time

A fictional novel about the granting of a special wish made by a highly regarded and successful young businessman.

Jason Darrow had found so much success just before his fortieth birthday, yet he was alone, unhappy, and in a mild state of depression. His private consulting firm was in such great demand, he could choose his next customer from a long list requesting his services. He could set his own start date for the next project and name his price for six weeks of examination.

Still, no amount of money, attention from beautiful women, booze or expensive hobby could replace the daily plunge into sadness. He hid his affliction from friends and foes with a steely passion. Jason was divorced, had no children and couldn't manage a serious relationship for more than a few months. His few close friends called him "the relationship killer". All he knew was that in his lifetime he had truly loved two women and married a third who he hoped he would grow to love. Every time a personal or business problem arose, he somehow managed to return to the failure of his relationships with first Marcie, then Rosa. He had fallen hard for Marcie McClain in college, only to have her reject his too deep and too soon professed love for her. Rosa had been different. The most beautiful woman he had ever seen cared about him, but he pushed her away over a silly argument. For twenty years, Jason Darrow had bemoaned, cursed and blamed the failure of these two relationships for his every serious problem.

The expected publish date for "If I Could Turn Back Time" is Fall 2022.

All these books are available on Amazon in e-book, and paperback versions.

Paperback copies can also be ordered at:

www.sidmicklepublications.com

where personalized copies are available.

Contact Sid Mickle at:

admin@sidmicklepublications.com

Table of Contents

Prologue

Chapter 1   The Beginning of a Strong Work Ethic

Chapter 2   How I Arrived at a Principled Company

Chapter 3   Outer Circle Products, 860 West Evergreen, Chicago, IL

Chapter 4   The Principle of Openness

Chapter 5   The Principle of Respect

Chapter 6   The Principle of Teamwork

Chapter 7   The Principle of Balance

Chapter 8   The Principle of Taking Responsibility

Chapter 9   The Principle of Risk Taking

Chapter 10 The Principle of Quality

Chapter 11 The Shared Areas of Environment/Attitude/Results

Chapter 12 Conclusion

Prologue

A few years ago, I was fortunate enough to work for a small, entrepreneurial company, Outer Circle Products, LTD, based in Chicago, IL. In this book, I detail how our owner implemented a dramatic change in the culture of our company. His idea was to establish a group of principles, developed by the employees, to guide every aspect of our business. This talented young man, Tom, took the time, spent the money necessary, and dedicated himself to building a great company environment.

I will review the creation of our principles and offer several examples of how they were followed in work situations. I provide a personal evaluation of the wonderful culture these principles helped us create. This writing is not a memoir of my work history, although I write a great deal about business events I experienced at Outer Circle. My goal is to explain the principles we employees created, discuss the guidelines attached to each of them, and provide real life examples of their execution and benefits.

Tom's leadership team supported his idea and committed to our cultural changes. They worked every day to create a thriving, principles focused, work environment. My direct manager, Larry, was the VP of Sales when I started my career there and he later became the company's President. He was one of the most talented and influential leaders I worked with in my career. Larry supported the cultural changes and lived the principles from the first day. He did this while managing a team in an office setting and an external field sales force. A sincere compliment I would offer to this manager, who became a close friend, is how I felt he was a "benevolent manipulator." He took the time to understand what I needed in order to perform well and moved me into solid business practices and leadership positions. With his support and direction, I became a better manager and a better person.

Our VP of Operations, Charlie, led the Chicago production team and worked well with other departments while practicing the principled culture. He was always direct, respectful, and energetic. He was passionate about what we were trying to do and willing to work hard to accomplish our goals. Being a former college athlete, Charlie hated excuses and did not allow half-hearted effort. He was a confidant motivator and an outstanding leader.

We had what I describe as a unique HR department manager. Stacey was fully committed to our principled culture. She was a person you could trust and share private concerns on any subject. However, she was not someone who felt the need to pat people on the head and tell them everything would be ok. If you asked for her opinion, you received a very honest answer. She became a close, wonderful friend, and I believe she also loved our cultural changes. However, she never shied away from "tough love" if it was needed.

The most important obligation to our culture was the requirement to respect everyone. We were a company of black, brown, and white individuals. We were of Asian, Hispanic, American and Canadian nationalities. We were gay, straight, and other sexual identities. None of these labels or qualifiers mattered, or determined an individual's value at our company. What mattered was your effort, dedication and ability to work with a diverse group of colleagues. The support of our principles, by every employee, afforded us the fair and equal conditions that made us unique and successful. In my forty-year business career, I never worked with a more dedicated and talented group of people. It is difficult to explain or describe the joy, growth, success and overall pride I felt in my company, my team and my work. After working in this new environment, no other job was as rewarding as my ten years at Outer Circle Products. The energy, passion and dedication I experienced there were extraordinary.

The idea behind this culture is easy to describe, but a difficult thing to understand. A principled culture demands a total and complete commitment to this new philosophy by every person in the company. It calls for an agreement to live the culture every day, in all situations, by every manager and member of the team. The benefits of this commitment are many, but the pure joy of loving what you do is the true payoff for workers in a principled culture.

This is a "how we did it" book about creating a company-wide work environment to support cultural changes necessary to make this complex environment sustainable. My experiences described herein are exactly as they happened. There are no phony stories, made-up or embellished successes to justify the practices I describe. The statements and facts offered are authentic, and I lived each of them mentioned here. This is a company very few people outside our business segment ever knew.

Outer Circle Products, LTD, was a Chicago based housewares company. We marketed items in the molded plastic music storage segment, the soft insulated cooler, and lunch kit retail segments. These were not well-known large categories, then or now. Our entry into these business segments added innovation, functionality and style. We increased the size of the product offering in each category and provided consumers with better choices for their needs.

It was exciting to watch our company revenue grow from approximately \$3M to over \$120M. From a small group of approximately twenty employees, we expanded to just under fifty full time employees in under ten years. It is my belief, as well as many of my former colleagues, that our principled environment and overall culture created the right conditions for this growth. We sold our products in these relatively small business segments dominated by major competitors like Rubbermaid, Igloo, and Coleman. There were also a few other small start-up companies and several direct import vendors. Competing against large organizations with huge sales teams and big marketing budgets made our task challenging. Early in the development of our business, our owner wanted to change our company dramatically. He felt this change would make our business something special, and make us more competitive. Still, I don't believe this was his primary motive. I believe he wanted a positive and dynamic change in how people worked and an environment that respected every individual. He created, implemented and supported a principled company environment, believing this step would make our team much stronger. He helped our team establish a culture that employees loved enough to keep it alive.

In other business cultures, strong managers can force employees to follow their individual rules and strategies. This was something our new and completely different culture worked to prevent. Tom wanted a culture created and executed by all employees in the company. It was a tremendous risk and a wonderful result.

I am convinced the principled work environment is the key to real growth for any company and for most every employee. Yes, employees, managers, owners and, to a great extent, your vendors, customers and competitors gain a significant benefit from a principled culture. While this book offers a blueprint on how to establish this type of environment, it is also a source of its reality and the story of its success. The basic business results of profitability, increased distribution and product innovation, and other accomplishments were measurable.

Like others, at the beginning of this process, I felt we would have a tough time changing our methods of doing business. I was fairly certain this much discussed cultural change was some type of new motivational strategy to reset our team and give everyone the energy we needed to compete in a small, crowded business segment. I fully expected our managers to return to established methods of telling people what to do, checking up on them and then dealing out criticism to those who fell short.

After three, week-long trips to Chicago working on the development of our specific set of principles, I understood it was more than I had expected. There was a feeling of hope in the room that we were being heard and actually influencing what was being created and agreed upon. I remember several late-night conversations at local watering holes about what was happening. The sales team, which I was a part of, was very skeptical. We thought the company would make a few changes to our daily interactions, and when the first challenge reached the highest level of managers, the company would fall back on old methods. After the first few doubtful weeks turned to months of strictly following the principles, those of us in the field often talked about what was going on inside the Chicago office. Since our owner was the originator of this new culture, he would not be the prime indicator of its reality. We wanted to see how the guys managing the company every day handled themselves. In our first meeting, we experienced interactions beyond what we expected.

Charlie, our VP of Operations, was a huge proponent of our culture change and a fierce supporter of the principled culture. His obvious support only left our boss, the VP of Sales, to confirm our doubts. When his first test arrived, which I will discuss later on, he showed us his commitment to our new way of working together. He practiced the principles while managing the internal employees along with an experienced and outspoken field sales team. I was convinced, and I threw my full support into learning how to work in a new and better business culture.

Changes like this one are not easily accepted or easily put in place. I remember much skepticism from friends in traditional businesses when I explained what we were doing with the Outer Circle Products culture. I also remember push back from people inside the company who didn't want to see any radical changes to their daily way of doing business. I watched talented people fight the cultural changes we set in place and eventually leave the company. I heard loud voices from other business leaders who said we were a gimmick and a joke. Those of us who experienced the best working environment in our careers laughed quietly and let them critique and diminish our methods. We proceeded with a dedicated, committed team and grew the business and profits. We also increased the confidence and improved the skills of our employees. I know there will be many experts in today's business who will scoff at this type of business environment. Those doubters do not interest or concern me. The success of our principled business culture was real and had a life changing, positive impact on most everyone involved. For me, it was like a fuel driving my desire to be better and make my team better.

These new practices differed from those of any company I worked for before. Our guidelines and expectations were motivating and positive. I was honestly excited to get to work every day. Even when I knew the events of the day were going to be difficult, I knew I was fully supported and not on my own. The requirement to do all I could to accomplish my goals was not a sense of pressure. I saw these challenges as an opportunity to perform. I don't have the words to describe the strong, positive feelings I had for our culture. All I can say is, the atmosphere there fit me well and gave me a confidence and level of success I never had before.

I am fully convinced almost every company, no matter the business segment they operate within, can create and implement a principled business culture. This incredible change to your daily environment will affect how your business operates every day. It can provide tremendous benefits to all aspects of your company and open the door to significant growth by every employee. Instead of tinkering with phrases, slogans and lofty words, I suggest a very detailed review of your existing culture with input from as many people as reasonably possible, and input from every department. If you can determine where your culture is falling short, you can identify and embrace changes to make your business more productive and efficient with a highly dedicated workforce.

The principles we supported at the one and only company I worked for with this type of approach and shared beneficial culture are:

Openness-Teamwork-Balance-Respect-Taking Responsibility-Risk Taking-Quality

In this writing, I offer a first-hand view of my experiences with a principled environment and attempt to explain how significant and beneficial the changes to our team were from the early days of developing and implementing our company principles. These are not simply words a company owner decided upon and posted on a flashy sign in our offices. Our team created and lived these principles by working together with our owner, managers and all employees. As you see, I choose the term employees instead of associates. I feel the term employee better reflects the people who work within a company instead of the term associates. Our goal was to be clear, genuine and direct in all our communication. This meant removing anything pretentious, insincere, or potentially viewed as a word-smithing exercises. We were employed to do different jobs by the company and the term employee fit us just fine. We objected to anything overstated, as hype, or not a real and honest practice. Everything we did regarding the establishment of our principles was an honest, respectful, and meaningful evaluation of our work activities. We spent the time necessary to fully understand the impact of the changes we were making throughout the company.

Like most of our team, I had a solid work ethic when I joined the company and I had twelve years of post-college, sales and marketing experience. I developed my personal work ethic through part-time jobs as a young man and furthered it with my experiences at Johnson & Johnson McNeil and Unilever Corporations' Ragu Food division. This work ethic helped me evaluate, understand, and fully commit to the idea of a principled environment.

I have tried to avoid any of the aforementioned "word-smithing", buzz word creation, or repeating of any other worthless, shallow and phony corporate speak. Catchy phrases, platitudes and ultra-positive, "I care more than anyone" statements are a hollow virtue signaling practice. These things might look great on a Facebook page or a LinkedIn post, but those things do nothing to help your company environment or business success. My goal is to show clear and honest examples of how to improve your company with a simple but extremely difficult cultural change. The creation process is straightforward, but the daily support of this new culture is challenging. I will attempt to explain how it can be developed, implemented, and executed daily.

I attempt to relate how other career positions were the foundation for my working life, and contrast those cultures with the principled environment. I learned many positive things in my former jobs and those lessons made me a better employee, manager and overall contributor at each step of my career. The principled culture experience gave me a roadmap of how to connect these lessons and set my personal style.

One thing I am proud of is the confirmation by former team members of my leadership and relationships with them. It is a rewarding moment when a person you have managed tells you they loved working with you. I have been fortunate to have several of them tell me they felt I cared about them and their families as much as their work performance. Most said I was tough, but fair, throughout our working relationship. With this managerial style, I formed long-time friendships with colleagues, customers and competitors by being respectful and interested in their lives and careers. My goal was to show how their input and emotional connection counted in our work together.

A wonderful fact I learned at the greatest company you never heard of, Outer Circle Products, was a simple statement at the close of our final initial meetings. When I told our owner I was excited about our changes, he had an interesting comment. He said, "If you can convince people their efforts and ideas really matter in how our company operates, and show how they contribute to our success, they will work harder than they ever have before." This is an accurate statement, and after ten years of incredible growth at this small company, I understood this place would be the best work experience of my career. Yes, the best job I ever had.

To be clear, my experience in this culture occurred years ago. This does not diminish the potential results or positive impact a principled culture could have on a business. The subject of this book is not a theory, it is not a simulation or short-term experiment. It was not a "controlled environment" with a pre-ordained result done to trick a workforce into working harder for the benefit of only the business owner. This complete and total change to the everyday interactions of a group of workers and their work environment was an expensive and risky move. It was done with a reasonably large group in a for-profit business which was not in a desperation mode. This step was taken to make a very solid company a great company.

The creation and daily practices of our principles was a leap of faith and a deep belief in the idea people want to be heard, and each of them can improve overall business results. These people want to have a positive impact on their company, the people around them, and themselves. I am writing about experiences I had during the ten years I spent with this great company. There is nothing in the passage of time or changes to the business world, making this wonderful culture less important today. The beneficial changes in personal interactions, management style and positive results are undeniable. I wrote this book to tell the story, discuss the process, and explain my personal experiences.

This Outer Circle Products style of cultural change may never be implemented in another company. If not, I honestly believe it is a loss for many businesses and employees. It is easy to understand there are many work environments needing this type of cultural change. Most successful businesses and management teams understand the need for a positive work environment. They understand how employees want to feel valued and want to be strong contributors. I am fully convinced they will react much better to a culture of responsibility than one of accountability. The core value of showing respect to everyone at all times is an unquestionable positive action and requirement.

It is important to understand that the benefits of these environmental changes are not a one-way street. Businesses will also benefit from the improvements made through better personal exchanges, innovation, and overall quality. There is also the benefit of freeing your team to challenge the status quo, take measured risks, and produce great results. My experience and firm belief are that implementation of a principled business culture is a winning situation for everyone involved.

I do not mean this book to be a sermon on my support of this culture or a lecture criticizing different methods and points of view. I can only reiterate how my career was positively impacted by this style. The examples and stories I tell in this book are real and happened in a successful, entrepreneurial, for-profit business. I can also say we had conflicts and failures, along with our success. We also had small groups and cliques which were closer to each other than other employees. The difference was these groups had no exceptions to the requirements of our principles. They still had the obligation to respect everyone all the time, and they received no special consideration.

I understand that many companies work hard to maintain a positive internal culture which benefits their employees. Likewise, some companies don't have a serious interest in any specific culture, but from time to time offer surface changes that don't make a difference or last. Those companies are usually more interested in profits and growth of market share. Other businesses have a simple, "do what we tell you or go away" culture and management philosophy. Those toxic environments are demeaning and harmful. People working in these conditions can experience bullying, manipulation, and often, serious harm to their self-esteem. These things are much worse than the simple description of "toxic work environments". They are conditions allowed by management which can do long-term harm to individual careers and damage families. It is easy to say, "Never stay in a toxic work environment", but it is altogether another thing for some people to make a change. There are situations where an employee may be at an age where a comparable job is not available. I have been in this position myself, and it is a terrible dilemma. I truly hope this book can have a positive influence on businesses concerned about their work environment.

Under the best conditions, work is hard. When I hear people say, "My workplace is like a big family", I hope this is true. Outer Circle was, in some ways, similar to a family setting, but it was still work. It would be a misunderstanding to think having a principled culture solves all problems and makes everyone happy. It does not. What it should do is absolutely require an unchanging level of respect for everyone. It should at all times strive to enforce reasonable guidelines which move everyone forward without unnecessary conflict, anxiety and mistreatment.

I want this book to explain clearly the benefits of a respectful, positive culture. There are many ways to find improvements, make important positive changes impacting employees and supporting company goals. Also, the specific principles I discuss here are not a sacred or a perfect list. Diverse groups of employees in various business segments need to establish their own principles or guidelines.

As you read this book, you will see several words and common themes repeated dozens of times. This is because they are not only critical to the understanding and life of the principled culture, they are a vital part of each principle. I repeat them here to show their importance and necessary practice in the principled environment. This was also the case when we were conducting the original principles creation meetings. Many of these words and themes were quoted often during the first few months of making them part of our daily routines.

We linked certain thoughts and concepts to every principle and contributed to building the final version of our principled business culture. This was a natural occurrence and not a predetermined method of creating value or importance during specific area of discussion. If our owner, over a three-week period, simply exposed us to a subliminal plan of his own thinking, he is more talented and brilliant than I believed back then. Still, I will agree our repetition and focus on key themes was absolutely intentional. We had to create a natural, unhesitating response of respecting everyone, having open and honest conversations and taking responsibility for all our actions, to get this major cultural change started and becoming our work standard.

In the final chapter, I attempt to summarize this process and build a flexible checklist to keep in mind in all stages of a cultural change. Then I discuss how individuals can create their own list of principles and make personal changes. My sincere hope is that this book causes the reader to think, evaluate their workplace and examine their own interactions within their current work environment.

Chapter 1

The beginning of a strong work ethic

I grew up in rural Alabama and, like most youngsters, I knew very little about the concept of work ethic. Still, I saw daily examples by most adults around me working hard and being fully invested in providing for their families. Every adult I knew or had contact with seemed to work hard and do all they could to make their families' lives and their own as good as possible. My parents worked in a local textile factory we called "the mill". After a few years of living in the company sponsored housing known to locals and mill workers as "the village", we moved into an old drafty rental house on a small farm. We were poor, but not poverty-stricken. I don't mean to overstate our limited financial situation or living conditions. We actually wore shoes, so none of the common and wrong hillbilly garbage and stereotyping was present, and we had fairly decent clothes. We were not hungry or in need of help, but were lacking in many areas. We were not in any form worldly or sophisticated. Our daily lives were busy, filled with obligations, mostly happy and, to us, normal. My folks worked hard to provide the necessities, and this left little money for anything else.

We weren't in the socioeconomic middle class, but we did just fine. I never felt poor or damaged by our living status as a kid, but I understood if I wanted to spend money, I needed a part-time job. There was no weekly allowance for me or my sisters, so the only option was a job. As teenagers, both my two sisters worked and with help from my dad, I got a Saturday job at a local service station, or as we called it, a filling station when I was twelve years old. Over the next four years, I worked at this place and then a larger and busier service station, ran a 500+ subscriber paper route and then worked part-time for the same textile company as my parents, Avondale Mills. I was very fortunate to work for honest, solid business owners who treated me well. All were demanding, and I worked hard for little pay, but I was safe and received the benefit of their experiences and leadership.

At fourteen years of age, I wanted a motorcycle. I wanted to ride around on my own, like many of my friends. Just as I was trying to decide how to convince my parents to agree to this idea, a perfect opportunity came my way. A local kid was running an eighty-subscriber paper route and seemed to make a good profit from this job. He wanted out of the job despite the money, so I began asking lots of questions. My appeal to my parents was that I could make enough money to pay for a motorcycle, have a little responsibility, with money left over. They were not big fans of my owning and riding a motorcycle, but everything else was appealing to them. After a few days of begging and whining, they agreed to talk with the parents of the kid running the route. We learned that this young guy was making about $30.00 profit per week but had a bad habit of spending the money he collected before paying the publisher for his daily allocation of one hundred and twenty Montgomery-Advertiser newspapers. This meant his parents were paying a sizeable portion of his costs and they wanted out of the newspaper delivery business. Less than a month after hearing about this job, I had my own small business and became the new local paperboy.

For almost a year, I got up at 4:00 am, sat on the sidewalk at Collins Drug Store in my hometown rolling newspapers, and then delivered them, seven days a week. The only negative to the job was dealing with customers who had to be visited directly to collect for their subscriptions. Most of my customers mailed payments to the company, but about twenty-five needed a personal visit to make their payment. This aspect of the job somewhat soured my customer service skills. As a young man, I heard every excuse you could imagine not to pay. I quickly learned how stopping service to them only meant I lost the past due payments, so I had to keep delivering and hounding them to pay their past due balance and still make a profit. Some of these customers eventually settled their account and others just ignored me until I gave up and stopped their deliveries. Even with this problem, by staying disciplined, I paid for my motorcycle, a brand-new Honda 90cc, covered my gas expenses, and saved a few bucks as well.

After a few months, I was an expert at slinging newspapers from my small blue motorcycle and learning how to manage the money the job created. During this period of time, a major change was taking place in the lives of most kids in my hometown. A new school was opening and I wanted to remain with my friends and continue playing football with my teammates on our successful junior high team. We were rising sophomores and this new school, Chambers Academy, was an expensive private school. There seemed to be no way I could make the move to this new school, since we didn't have the funds for tuition. After several conversations with my mother, she came up with an idea to earn the money needed. She suggested I take over a much larger paper route to earn enough to make the move to the new school. How she learned about this opportunity, I do not know. I was eager to do most anything to solve the financial problem, so I agreed and we took over the new route. Since I could not manage this larger business alone, she agreed to help me run the now four hundred eighty subscriber combined route.

Frequently in this book, I mention how lucky I was to work with great mentors during my career. While each of them had a strong and usually positive impact on me, none came close to my parents, especially my mother. While my dad was the disciplinarian and somewhat distant, she was a constant example of love, faith and hard work. I am not sure how she woke up at 3:30 am, helped me deliver papers until 6:00 am and then worked an eight-hour shift at her full-time job. I have no words to describe the love and support I received in order for me to move to the new school with my friends.

My new paper route had the original eighty customers from the Montgomery-Advertiser and would now add over four hundred deliveries of the Columbus (GA) Ledger-Inquirer newspaper. My mother bought a used VW, and we altered the interior to accommodate the nearly six hundred daily papers, which included the stock for several newspaper boxes. For two years we operated this business, paid our expenses, paid my tuition and saved approximately 50% of the fees necessary for my senior year tuition. The work was hard on me and I was a young, strong kid. I can't imagine the effort and toll it took on my mother. Somehow, the desire to provide something I wanted and most likely needed outweighed the work required. I am comfortable saying this change was something I needed. I left a deteriorating public school system and found myself in a much better situation. Had I known how much tougher the school work would be, I might not have been so eager to make this change. I credit my three high school years at Chambers Academy, which is still in operation today, with providing a solid base education. I learned how to write better, speak better, and follow a strict set of behavioral rules. My time there was balanced and filled with discipline. It was one of the best decisions our family ever made.

When we left the paper delivery business, it was a memorable time in my life. I can't imagine what a relief it was for my mother. Very few days stand out as happily as the day we turned this business over to a new delivery service. I missed the money the work provided, but returning to a normal schedule and healthier life was a simple choice.

This example of hard work stayed with me for a long time. The work ethic my parents possessed was shown to me practically, and their example showed I needed to work hard myself. No other jobs, except for a short stint as a roofer, then a loader on a hay bailing team, were as physically demanding. Even the three months doing the same job as my father at Avondale Mills was not quite as physically draining as the early morning paper route. Perhaps my parents went along with this tough work experience to teach me the value of getting a solid education. Even if this was not their plan, it was the lesson I learned. I also learned there could be truth to the adage of, "what doesn't kill you, makes you stronger". The lesson for me was I had to work hard to get certain things I wanted. The result was a firm foundation on the concept called a work ethic.

At sixteen, I moved from my giant paper route and took a summer job at the mill where my parents worked. Avondale hired the kids of their workers for either ongoing part-time or summer jobs. It was a well-known fact that if your folks worked there, they would find a job for you. I was happy to have this job and be able to earn spending money without feeling like I would fall asleep if I sat down for a few minutes. I worked on the weekend clean-up crew, the yard-mowing crew, and as a night watchman during the summer of my junior year of high school. My parents had worked at the mill all my life, and I knew most employees at this company.

My best description of the job is basic, unskilled work, providing the opportunity to earn the little money I needed. When I say a little money, that is exactly what I mean. My first hourly pay rate was $1.65 per hour. In 1971, $1.65 an hour was about as good as any kid in our town could find. I would play football on Friday night, then drive to the mill on Saturday morning for my cleanup crew shift from 6:00 am until 2:00pm. I would be stiff, sore and dead tired when I got there, but I never had pressure from anyone. I think they made sure we had a way to earn a little money and have some responsibility with little pressure. Only a couple of the shift supervisors were sticklers for being busy most every minute of a shift. Others kept an eye on us, but didn't mind if we slacked off at times. I learned a lot about how to work with unique personalities and various managers at this place. Since I knew almost everyone working there, the job transition was easy.

Being one of the goofy kids pretending to work around the adults, I also felt the sting of a few practical jokes. There were many characters working at the mill in those days. Some were old, or at least seemed old. Some were young, and others were just people I crossed paths with on a semi-regular basis. The plant manager, Mr. James Sellers, was a great guy who cared about his team and dealt with issues as fairly as possible. Mr. Sellers was someone I looked up to all my life. He was the one guy I could never BS. He would put up his hand and say, "Just stop", whenever I started some stupid explanation or excuse. He wanted the best for me, and he stayed after me to do well in high school and college. After my freshman year, I had some tough personal times and dropped out of college. When I returned home, I took another job at the same local textile mill. Each time I saw Mr. Sellers, he reminded me my job at the mill was temporary, and I should work there only to get back to college. I am sure he never knew how many times I thought about his advice, discipline, and support.

It seemed to me the workers, supervisors, office staff and lowest ranked person on the worker chain got along great at the mill. There were very few exceptions to the rule of getting along. Life for these folks was tough and the very few, unnecessary, poor attitudes got called out and dealt with quickly. I would say the work force was thirty percent black and the rest white, with no other diversity. James Sellers was an active and strong leader of this group when racial tensions were high in the southeast. I never heard one person say a bad word about him. He was direct, demanding and wanted to see a strong effort from everyone in his facility. If there was a problem during a shift, he would go onto the work floor and do anything needed to resolve the issue. If an employee had a problem, he listened, gave advice and if he could, helped them. He watched over our small group of part-time high school workers with an eagle eye and demanded discipline and effort, but tempered those things to fit a bunch of young, inexperienced kids. He was not someone you could fool or take advantage of often. However, when we were beat up from football games, he would pull our group off demanding work and put us on a job we could manage and get us through the day. Mr. Sellers was like another parent. I trusted him and felt he always wanted the best for me. There is not much more an employee could expect from a manager. He was another one of the great mentors I was fortunate enough to work for early in my career.

The mill allowed our part-time kids group to work an eight-hour shift on Saturdays and come in for four hours on Sunday doing much of the same work. If you wanted more, they would find another four to eight hours for you during the week after school. During the summer, we packed yarn when the first shift guys didn't finish the task and we mowed the entire property. Some of my best times there were during long, hot nights working as a night watchman. This job was a twelve-hour shift from 6:00 pm to 6:00 am. I recall sitting outside the mill in my car, often listening to Cincinnati Reds' games on the radio. I also remember the struggle to stay awake after the 2:00 am security check rounds until my 6:00 am shift end. I carried a time clock around the mill property, checking on six to seven locations. At each one, I slipped long keys into it to record my hourly rounds. It was boring, lonely and sometimes scary being there alone all night. Every time I went into the huge, dark cotton and finished goods warehouses, I got this "What else is in here", feeling. I had no supervision, but had to stay awake and make my rounds every hour without fail. It was one of my first lessons on self-discipline and self-motivation. The job helped me understand how to work properly even if there was no manager around to check on me. The mill management expected me to perform a certain task and if I didn't do it properly, the company had no place or need for me.

My greatest lesson and very real, life altering experience took place at Avondale Mills in 1974. I was young and struggling with some things many young people found hard to manage. I was angry at myself for failing at college football, involved in a terrible relationship and, overall, not a good person to be around. I was nineteen years old and after dropping out of college, I needed to pay for my car and a tiny apartment. The economy was in recession and jobs were scarce. As I mentioned, I returned to the mill and took a job doing the same work my father had done for thirty years. I could not believe how hard the work was every minute of the day. It was hot, intense, and I was part of a team effort to get production numbers from the spinning frames. In this department, I had the job of "doffer", with a set of assigned frames in this textile facility. After taking the full bobbins of yarn off and dropping a fresh one onto the spindles, I had to "start-up" the spinning frame with a start/stop button and a foot-peddle. The yarn ends had to stay attached and wind around the fresh bobbins. Every time I started a frame, about half the ends broke and the female workers in the department called, "spinners", had to rush over and reattach them. They hated working with me because I could not get this done well. I only lasted approximately two months at this hard labor.

The lesson I mentioned was like my paper route experience. Those laborer jobs were not the key to a better life. I knew I had to get back into school, get a degree and get away from this dead end, back-breaking work. My parents were not disappointed I didn't last in the mill, especially my dad. I am sure he wanted me to avoid the hard work he had done for years and do something better with my life. The fact these jobs would soon disappear was not my reasoning. Like most people in our area, I thought the mill would be there forever. Soon, its closing would cripple the local economy and move more people nearer to poverty. I was one of the fortunate ones from the local hourly wage group. I was young enough to make a change, find my way back to college, and later on, enjoy a well-paying and rewarding career. Most of the adults I worked with at the mill moved into farm or timber work, if they were young and healthy enough. Others lived on social security, part-time wages or support from churches or government programs. No one I knew ever received a dime from the pension funds they had contributed to for years, including my mother and father. Sometimes, work ethic was not enough to find success.

After college, I discovered the differences in work in blue-collar and white-collar jobs. The work I did after college was never easy, but instead of physical work, these positions required more mental effort to develop skills like planning, organization and follow-up. I traded a world of sweat for stress, anticipation, and very often, anxiety. I experienced both forms of work and learned to appreciate the differences.

My years with large corporations like Johnson & Johnson's McNeil CPC division and the Ragu division of Unilever Corporation were like my early days in the working world. I received excellent training and was guided by experienced and dedicated managers at every position in both companies. Like all fresh graduates entering large corporations, I was green as grass and unsure of my ability to manage most any part of my new business assignment. To complicate matters, I was a field sales person working from a home office. There was no manager near me for weeks on end. I was in an assigned market, trained and expected to work without supervision each day. No one noticed what time I left home or returned. This lack of supervision and personal responsibility was the undoing of many people in our field sales business. Without the requirement to operate from a central location each day and receive assignments and direction, several very talented people developed bad habits and eventually failed. This was something I saw at McNeil occasionally, and with other field sales managers. The key to my growth and development was my work ethic and the realization of the great opportunity I had. No one needed to tell me to plan my work day the night before, or get up and go to work. I wanted to be successful, and I wanted my managers to have confidence in me.

My first manager at McNeil told me not to fall into the trap of taking afternoons or days off. He explained how I could do this with no one finding out in the short term. Then he let me know a lack of presence in my assigned retail stores and direct selling accounts would become obvious to a talented manager. If he and I were in retail stores during a multi-day field trip and I was not recognized, the reason would be easy to see. If very few people in the direct accounts knew or were familiar with me, he would quickly understand I was not doing my job properly. The only way to have a presence in the assigned markets was to work those markets consistently.

My unit manager, Bill, was very clear in his direction. Managing my territory was my responsibility alone, and I was being paid to do my job in the most professional way possible. His boss, my district manager, also gave me clear direction. One night, after a full day of retail and direct account meetings, he gave me some sound advice. He warned me to never risk my reputation and my job by making dumb decisions. He told me face to face he knew all the tricks in manipulating an expense account or not being in the field every day. His exact words were, "Don't make me fire you for faking a $100.00 expense account entry. Do your job as if Bill or I are with you every day and you will be successful". Next, he mentioned how lucky I was to have my position and be a member of his team. He told me to never worry about taking an hour or two during the week for an important personal issue. Adding, "Just make the time up in your office later that night, the next day, or over a weekend. Treat the company's money and your time like it was your own business and gain our trust". As I have said often, I worked for plain speaking, honest and dedicated managers at most every point of my career.

My original unit and district managers moved on to other assignments in less than two years. I was incredibly fortunate to have another influential business manager take over. Paul took charge of the Jacksonville district and became one of the most important influences in my life. This guy was tough, knew the business well and demanded effort from our team. When he arrived, he laid out the changes he expected in our activities and our performance. He let everyone know he was in charge and from there, we would follow his plan or we could seek employment elsewhere. He wanted the team fully committed to his program, or he was prepared to replace anyone who did not want to accept the changes required. Paul was clear, direct and expected us to follow his plan. He was available to everyone and spent field time in every market in the District. I was fortunate to have him see some potential in me, and he worked to develop my modest skills as much as possible.

From the beginning, there was a normal push back on the changes he demanded. As a group, we had grown accustomed to the previous management style and did not want to accept the change he represented. Those of us who had seen success through our existing practices were not eager to make the changes Paul demanded. Like several others, I felt he was much too critical of everything I was doing. He reviewed, critiqued and changed most every part of my sales plan for the large customers in my markets. I had moved to Jacksonville to take over the largest territory by dollar volume in the district. I had met all my sales and promotional goals, so I was not happy to hear he wanted me to make a lot of changes. What was really happening was a serious and extensive review of my selling skills and leadership potential. He challenged me in ways I had not expected, and there were times I felt he wanted me to resign. I took his attention as a direct challenge to my personal commitment and sales skills. My competitive nature took over, and I worked harder than ever to show him I knew what I was doing. I took every opportunity to show him my ability and value to the company. As soon as I committed to being successful, no matter what he threw at me, I was on my way to more personal growth.

Over the next few months, I did exactly what he wanted, and I listened to his advice and direction. Paul taught me how to work smarter, plan better, and give great effort every day. Then he recommended me for the district trainer position. This was the required first step of being considered for management at McNeil, and the move surprised me. After gaining this additional responsibility, Paul spent even more time with me and had me fully prepared for my first trainee. He didn't put me in the position and say "You figure this out". We worked together almost every day for two weeks before my first training assignment. When the training session began, I was ready, well prepared, and successful. We had long conversations about the importance of my work with the new hires and about what I should learn as they assigned more trainees to me. Paul let me know his expectations and explained exactly what I needed to do to advance my career and move into management.

Like my old boss in the textile plant, he was never willing to accept any excuses or BS. There were times I wanted to be far away from him in my career, but as I grew and developed, I realized he was an incredible and valuable asset. I quickly learned my best course would be to listen, trust his direction, and work hard. After two years of working with Paul, I advanced to the Unit Manager level and was soon promoted to my first district manager position. To this day, I count him as one of my greatest mentors and best friends. I know he is only a phone call away should I need him. As you can easily see, the company gifted me with great mentors and teachers during my time there.

Without really knowing it, I accepted change, trusted, and took the risks associated with more responsibility while I worked with McNeil. The same was true with my career at Unilever. My move to this company meant I could return to Jacksonville, be close to my kids, and enjoy a doubling of my current salary. Still, the biggest change was to have my first taste of an entrepreneurial sales approach.

At Unilever, I was the fourth member of a special Ragu Foods sales team charged with selling a food item to accounts not in the food segment. It was a strange thing to work for a major food company and sell our items to the "non-foods" classes of trade. We worked with drug chains, warehouse clubs, drug wholesale customers and a few major convenience store chains. Since we called on non-traditional classes of trade, we had to create promotional plans separate from the team selling into the grocery business segment. This change exposed me to being more creative and not simply following a marketing plan. The different approach clearly showed me how little I knew about creating a sales plan. I understood the accounts and the basics of selling, but I was inexperienced in building customer specific marketing programs. Our team was very successful and after a few months, I had success as well. This job was my first experience working with brokerage companies who sold our items to our customers.

This job was challenging and exposed me to a very different method of selling. I noticed a different culture within our small group. We were under the management policies and style of the Ragu Division, but our small group adapted a new method of communicating and sharing information. As I looked back on those years, I saw it as a similar environment to the one we created at Outer Circle. To be successful, we had to trust each other and communicate openly to meet our individual and team goals.

I describe my two years at Ragu Foods as a fresh look at how to do business. It was an exceptional experience, since I worked closely with a manager who was much more interested in results than power. He wanted to see our group accomplish our sales and distribution goals, but also wanted each of us to grow and try new methods. He wanted us to be free from the idea of a manager looking for accountability and have us take responsibility for everything we did. Lee trusted us to work with little supervision while he managed his own accounts and the overall business. For the first time, I felt an entire team could be comfortable trying new things and not being called on the carpet if we made a mistake.

This new situation lasted only a few years. They merged our Ragu division into the TJ Lipton company, and I was out of a job. What seemed like a terrible situation at the time was really the next step in finding the best job I held in my entire career. Lee told me I had six months to find a new job, and if more time was needed, he would ask for an extension. Within two months, I was moving to Outer Circle Products. He made sure my exit was smooth and fair. He paid me a full quarterly bonus even though I left during the middle of the quarterly bonus period. He was a demanding leader and required a strong effort from everyone. In return, he respected us and gave us his full support. Lee was another great mentor I was privileged to work with.

With these two large company experiences, I was well-trained, knowledgeable and prepared to do more. I learned how to work in a political environment and navigate the various cliques and power structures that existed in both. I saw people damage their career by not knowing how to manage those things well. There were times someone pushed back against the wrong manager or pushed too hard. When this happened, you could be labeled as a problem or difficult to manage employee. Others didn't take part in late-night drinking sessions after work, or took part and were sluggish the next day. With these so-called missteps, their careers suffered. They were not considered team players or strong enough for the job. It didn't matter how these things had nothing to do with their talent or ability, their only mistake was crossing the wrong person.

I once had a terrible experience with a salesperson who remained loyal to the district manager I replaced. She decided to report how I ran the business to this former manager and complain about the changes I had made and my leadership. These things happen with leadership changes, and I knew she was not happy with me. I met with her and tried to address her concerns, but she remained unhappy and difficult. Instead of trying to work things out and have more conversations, she reported what she felt were mistakes and mistreatment to her former manager. Again, crap happens, and I couldn't control this behavior. The one thing that was unacceptable was exaggerating, followed by flat out lying about certain events and asking this former manager to intervene with me. When this guy called, I was not surprised and expected him to pass on the information as a heads-up. Instead, he went on the attack, relying on misinformation, and accused me of mistreating this employee. I was shocked and pissed off, but I continued to listen. When he said, "My sources in the district tell me you are doing a terrible job", the conversation turned unpleasant. In a clear, loud voice, I explained how wrong it was for him to have sources in my group, but much worse to listen to them and criticize me.

With a detailed record of my work with this territory manager, I asked for a meeting with the regional manager to clear the air. His review with other members of my team made the two of them look foolish and earned a strong rebuke, or so I was told. From there, she and I continued to work together, but never had a productive relationship. The other manager refused to speak with me as long as I remained with the company. This was an excellent decision since the situation was ridiculous, out of line and changed nothing. I hated this type of political BS and bullying. This type of power play and others forced people to take crap from someone who considered themselves "a boss". Not really a talented leader or manager, but a title which required submission and respect. This type of leader is a disaster and creates an awful business environment. Does this situation fit the popular description of a toxic environment? I am not sure about the specific definition, but it is truly stupid, hierarchical and, worse than anything, disrespectful.

There is no doubt many of these things are part of your career, and fair or not, you must adapt. It is never fun to work for a manager who has "failed upward" and pushes people around based on their title. Instead of managing people, they threaten them with their rank and do absolutely nothing to benefit the employee or the company. I never had a problem with authority at any level and followed direction the best I could. With that said, I longed to find a company that valued everyone, respected them fully and tried to connect their growth and development with that of the overall company.

Chapter 2

How I Arrived at a Principled Company

As I mentioned, I worked for Johnson & Johnson McNeil for ten years. We were the manufacturers and distributors of the Tylenol* brands. I started my career there as an over-hire, meaning there was no open position for me, but the company liked me well enough to hire me. They sent me to the Ft. Lauderdale/North Miami Beach market immediately after graduation. My responsibility was 320 retail stores and ten Shoppers Drug Mart drug stores as my direct buying customer base. I received excellent and continuous training at the corporate level and from talented field managers. I was very fortunate to work for a great company like Johnson & Johnson. From this small and unimportant over-hire position, I moved six times in ten years and rose to the District Manager position within the company. This was how the business operated in those days. If you were not willing to move to the next assignment, your career stalled and most of the time, ended within a few months.

I experienced two Tylenol* tampering incidents during the first six years of my career. The first incident was national news as some maniac killed seven people in Chicago with Tylenol Extra Strength Capsules contaminated with cyanide. More than once during that episode, I felt our company and my career would soon disappear. However, over the next few months, I took part in one of the most incredible and well-planned crisis management cases and a remarkable marketing comeback. There were many times during the crisis I was not sure we would survive. The press tore us apart in the early days and wild rumors spread across our customer base several times. Early in this crisis, the President of McNeil appeared on the Donahue Show and laid out our case as a safe and solid business who had their goods used by a deranged maniac. This appearance marked a turning point in the understanding of what had happened, and we soon heard about a plan to return our brands to retail stores.

The first step in rebuilding our brand was to fly the entire company into Dallas for a national sales meeting. In those days, men and women traveled dressed in business suits, and carrying our popular Hartman briefcases. The hotel lobby had enough "Johnston & Murphy, Gucci and Nine West" dress shoes to fill a shopping mall. When I arrived at our hotel, I found my best friend Mario playing the piano in the open lobby with a drink close at hand. The entire sales and marketing team needed to visit with each other, vent, speculate and hope for better days. That is exactly what we did. At 1:00 am, the hotel bar closed, and we were directed to a private hospitality suite to continue our conversations. Management must have felt we had all been isolated, confused by many events, and worried enough to keep the suite open all night. I never made it back to my room after dropping off my bag and wore the same clothes to the opening presentation the next morning. My friend Mark and I went directly from the company suite to the first session of the day.

ABC news correspondent Howard K. Smith opened our meeting, and we spent the day learning how we would go about rebuilding our brand. After a general session recapping what had happened, we reviewed the steps we would take to begin our recovery. We learned each of us would have a business style checkbook at our homes when we returned and would be tasked with contacting all our customers. We would write each customer a check for the inventory returned by customers or pulled from shelves by their staff. We would also complete a shipping label for each box of merchandise, and it would be picked up at no cost and shipped to a facility in New Jersey. Every box received would be incinerated with no thought if someone had tampered with it or not.

We departed Dallas with some hope, but most of us felt we would be a minor brand in the market for years to come. Since I had the largest customers in the district, their number was small, with only four accounts. Winn Dixie was a breeze, and I had a great conversation with the buyer. He hoped we would come back in a big way. He explained something I had not really considered during the crisis. He told me he had a big hole in his sales and profit plan with no Tylenol* on store shelves and wanted to know everything I could tell him about our next steps. From that day, my buyer, Mr. Allen, and I had a much closer and stronger business relationship. The crisis actually made us more like business partners instead of a somewhat adversarial pair. Things went well with Certified Grocers in Ocala and they too wished us the best in returning to the market. My large drug wholesaler, Lawrence Pharmaceutical, had all their inventory packed and labeled before I arrived at their warehouse. It seems drug recalls were nothing new to them and they were fairly confident we would return to being a strong brand. The president of this company told me we had the advantage of an effective and high-quality product. Then he added the fact we spent millions of dollars on television advertising and physician detailing. To me, it was so far, so good.

This left me with one last meeting with my largest customer, Sav-A-Stop Wholesale Distributing. This company serviced and supplied thousands of convenience stores and small, independent retailers. When I met with my buyer to discuss payment for his inventory, he told me our brand would not exist within a year. He was not trying to attack our company or me. This was truly what he felt would result from the death of seven people who ingested an over-the-counter medication and died. I did not argue or push back against the opinions of my customers. My direction was to handle any problems with the returned merchandise as quickly as possible. The general plan was to write a check and take the returned goods out of their facilities.

After this brief conversation, he took me to his main warehouse where the returns were located. I describe what I saw there as being like the scene in "Raiders of the Lost Arc" when the crate holding the Arc was being rolled into a giant warehouse with thousands of similar containers. The Sav-A-Stop warehouse had large boxes, sitting two by two, the length of the main aisle. Box after box of every brand of Tylenol* items were returned and sitting on the floor. My buyer gave me a printout of what had been returned and the total was just over $1.0M, at cost.

I wasn't surprised, I was absolutely stunned. There were thousands of individual boxes of items other than capsules. They had Sine-Aid*, Co-Tylenol*, Adult Liquid medication and Tylenol* in tablet form in the product mix. I was expecting to only return capsule items since they were the only product form used in the tampering. When I explained this to my buyer, he insisted I get everything out of his warehouse immediately. I asked him to allow me to make a call to my boss to sort things out. He agreed, but added, "All this crap is leaving my building and never coming back."

I called my boss, Dave, and explained the situation. His reply was quick and unemotional. He only said four words, "Write him a check". I told him the buyer had refused to repack the merchandise in the boxes we supplied at no cost. Again, he said, "Write the check and tell him we will pick the goods up tomorrow. I will call transportation and get an expedited truck for the shipment. When you leave the building, give me a call." This was the first and only time I have written a check for such a large amount of money. I handed the buyer our check, we shook hands, and he said, "Good luck". When I called Dave later on, he explained how the company knew there would be customers who needed more exceptions than others. We could not debate the details. We would do everything we could to take care of our customers and return soon with an improved product line.

Over the course of the next few weeks, we shipped millions of dollars of inventory to the New Jersey facility and burned it. Shortly after this step, our operations team came up with a heat-sealed neck ring for all our capsule items and we glued the ends of all packages closed. To open the product, you needed to practically remove the closure tabs. From there, we held another national sales meeting to re-launch the capsule items in our product line. Almost every customer was pleased with the thirty-three percent discount and our marketing support of $1.00 off instant coupons for consumers, and millions in TV advertising. In a matter of weeks, our brand returned to retail shelves in every major market.

To support our wholesale customers, we offered an additional $1.00 per dozen allowance. This special deal was called a PM or "push money" allowance to help them push items from their warehouse into retail stores. I thought it was a significant step since my largest customer, the previously mentioned Sav-A-Stop Distributing, was a wholesale distributor. I did not know this step would lead to one of the most difficult and tense meetings I ever attended. To my surprise, they accepted our plans, gave me a large order and were anxious to get our product line into their customers' stores.

About two weeks after we shipped a $950K order to Sav-A-Stop with the $1.00 per dozen PM allowance, I listened to a message on my home office recorder from my former unit manager, Bill. He had been promoted to the Eastern Region Manager position and managed the K-Mart account. I had great respect for Bill and his business practices. I knew him well and after the opening sentence of his message, I knew we had a big problem. His first words were, "What the hell are you and Paul doing with Sav-A-Stop"? This professional, calm, respectful man was as angry as I had ever seen him. He wanted me to call him as soon as I got the message, so I called right away. Bill explained the details, and the longer he spoke, the angrier he became. I did not think he was angry at me, but I knew he was frustrated and had been embarrassed in front of his largest customer. Soon I learned the details of this problem. Sav-A-Stop had made an offer to pass on the $1.00 PM per dozen, directly to K-Mart. This was a tactic they used to attempt a takeover of the OTC medication business at K-Mart stores. Adding the $1.00 per dozen PM discount provided an additional $6.00 per case discount. Their selling price was reduced well below the sales price Bill could offer directly.

Within a few hours, my boss, the Jacksonville District Manager, our boss, the Southern Region Manager, and his boss, the National Sales Manager, were all involved in the conversation. Our region manager called the account and they readily confirmed making the offer. Their thought was we had nothing to say about how they used the additional discount. However, the promotional contract clearly stated, "To be used only with existing retailers serviced by the wholesaler before the product recall". Less than a week later, we scheduled a meeting at their corporate office. Paul and I were concerned with the fallout from this issue, but our National Sales Manager, Jack, reassured us. He was confident we could work out a solution and avoid any long-term problems.

Jack understood the situation and did not believe my boss and I were at fault. I was still a territory manager/trainer, and the lowest ranked member of the delegation attending this meeting. Paul and I had assembled presentation binders and a large flip chart with details of the promotion and its limits. At the meeting, the four of us sat on one side of a large conference room table, opposite five Sav-A-Stop participants. They brought in the two-person buying team, two VPs of Merchandising, and the company president. I handed out sales binders and moved to the front of the room and extended my fancy metal pointer to highlight key points on my oversized flip chart.

Before I finished my opening statement regarding page one, a Sav-A-Stop VP stood, then slammed the binder on the table. I watched the bound document slide the length of the table and fall at my feet. His reaction alone was shocking, but much worse was what he did next. He pointed to me and said, "You are a lying son of a bitch", and then pointing at my district manager, Paul, said, "And, you are a lying son of a bitch"! Then he angrily screamed at all of us for trying to tell them how to run their business. I was too angry and shocked to say anything right away, but Paul didn't sit still. He went right back at the guy and said he was out of line. It was then that our national sales manager turned to Paul and waved his hand to stop. Then he picked up his briefcase, opened it, and as he was putting away my presentation said, "Sid, thank you for putting this material together". Then he closed his case, stood, and calmly told the Sav-A-Stop president to call him if he wanted to have a professional conversation. As he turned to leave the room, their president said, "Jack, can you and I speak together outside?" The two left the room and the rest of us remained sitting at the table. My heart was pounding, and I was as angry as I had ever been in my brief business career. Paul and I glared at the VP who had called us liars, not saying a word. I noticed my buyer sitting nervously with his head lowered at the end of the table. It was the most uncomfortable five minutes I had experienced so far in my McNeil career.

The two senior managers returned to the room and said they had reached an agreement. We packed our materials and didn't say a word until we reached my company car. Jack told us he had explained the rules of the promotion and the Sav-A-Stop president agreed to pull their offer to K-Mart. He then said he was proud of how all of us had handled the personal attack by the Sav-A-Stop VP. His feeling was the outburst was meant to force us into a bad situation and distract from the subject of the meeting which was the contract. Then he said, "I'm starving, Sid. Where are you taking us to lunch?" That was it. There was no more conversation about the meeting.

I learned about being cool in a tense and difficult situation from the events of this meeting. I was incredibly impressed with how Jack handled himself and took all the pressure off the rest of us. The subject never came up again with anyone, including my buyer, during my next two years managing the account. My old boss, Bill, was happy with the outcome and pleased with how we supported his position. However, Paul and I had several cocktails over a detailed recap of the meeting after dropping off our senior managers at the airport.

At McNeil, we didn't have a principled business culture like what I will explain here, but our management team fully supported me. This difficult situation and my preparation helped me earn respect from these managers. This contentious meeting turned into a positive event and helped my career advance.

In the weeks after our product launch, we not only returned our brand to a leadership position, but grew the business beyond our market share when the incident occurred. I witnessed first-hand the power of open and honest communications with the media, our consumers, direct account customers, and the FDA. I saw how a strategic marketing plan could restore consumer confidence in a brand which had been used as a weapon, and rebuild a company's reputation.

My last position at McNeil was managing the Atlanta District and being responsible for a fourteen-member sales team. We handled the Wal-Mart/Sam's Club business, the largest distributor in the US, Mass Merchandisers, along with approximately one hundred other customers. We were the largest district by volume in the company and responsible for sales of over $120M annually. While managing this team, we won two National Sales Managers awards as the best performing district in sales volume against our quota or forecast. I was one minor cog on a gigantic wheel in the McNeil business structure. Like many successful junior managers, I thought I was an excellent businessman and district manager. In reality, I didn't know my ass from my elbow about how a business actually functioned. The company provided $35M in television advertising, couponing, and physician detailing to generate sales revenue. In our sales positions, we were simply caretakers of our local retail and direct buying customers. If we did our jobs well every day, we could add incremental sales in every market. Those incremental sales provided additional income via bonus opportunities, and sometimes this recognition could lead to career advancement.

Another thing I learned as a young territory manager, along with the importance of meeting your sales forecast goals, was to be buttoned up with all administrative tasks. This meant long hours in my in-home office at night and on weekends to get everything in order, and to be able to explain where your business plan was at all times. I took my manager's direction to heart and dedicated myself to his plan. I took pride in organizing my paperwork, sales tracking, direct customer headquarters penetration, and even my sales material organization in my company car. To me, it was simple. All these things really made my job easier and helped me sell more goods.

I remember a conversation with Bill one day in Fort Lauderdale at a Publix retail location. I opened my trunk to take out my sales bag and complete a retail store call. Bill commented he had never seen a more organized set up. I had the latest merchandising, display and sample materials organized in my company car. I thanked him and let him know if the company was going to be good enough to provide a car for me to drive and maintain, I could at least set it up properly. I think this trait and my competitive nature led him to have confidence I could develop my skills enough to become a sales trainer. I always felt my practice of being organized and the pride to repeat it every day led to my becoming a manager at McNeil.

Several of my larger customers often said our sales team was a collection of clones. We all looked the same, managed the business the same, and followed the company sales and marketing line as one voice. There was no entrepreneurial thinking at McNeil as it was not wanted or needed. We received a company marketing/sales plan and were expected to implement the strategy without question. I don't mean this as a criticism; I mean it as a compliment to the depth and execution of our corporate planning.

After being recruited away to the Unilever Corporation and its Ragu Foods division, I worked under a similar but slightly different type of planning and marketing program. They gave us a bit more latitude on how to build custom sales promotions for our various customers, but those programs still had to fall within corporate guidance and meet certain standards. Those things are a business reality. Every company must have a solid business plan and provide a sales, marketing or operational plan which fits and supports those assigned standards. I also understand most corporations do not fit or operate as entrepreneurial style companies. Even with this reasonable fact, it does not prevent any company from creating and supporting a principled business culture. I would guess many businesses would say they already have a similar style of environment. This is an easy thing to say when you really don't understand the major differences. I also feel it is natural for management to fear a loss of control in following a principled business culture. When the culture is properly managed, this is not a legitimate concern, but it is understandable.

A Principled Environment doesn't mean a "free for all" in behavior, tactics or strategy. It means the entire group is deeply involved with the company plans, are open to change, and invested in personal and company success. This involvement requires everyone to understand the obligation of contributing ideas and making suggestions. It does not mean you can be upset or whine when your suggestions or ideas are not accepted or implemented. Managers in a principled company must still manage. They must give direction, require compliance and move their teams toward the completion of the company plan. All managers in a principled environment have the advantage of open and honest input from every employee and the obligation to support an environment focused on making everyone better and accomplishing common goals.

The biggest benefit I had working with these two corporate giants was excellent training, large television advertising budgets and entry into the largest retailers in the country. Those things were valuable and made me a much better salesperson and manager. However, something was missing. There was no positive employee culture at either company. Our input wasn't wanted on strategy, and we didn't comment on or evaluate marketing outside our assigned territories. We were feet on the ground in an assigned market and expected to perform there with little concern beyond those borders.

After my three positive and enjoyable years of work at Unilever, I understood and did my work in a new style of doing business. I enjoyed being able to create custom promotional plans for my customers. The corporate downsizing and job loss seemed like a terrible situation when it arrived, but it was really the next truly great opportunity in my career. This change forced me to search for a new job. What I discovered was a completely new work environment and level of development both professionally and personally, beyond my imagination.

As I began my job search, I wanted to find something close to the experiences I had at Unilever. My first taste of an entrepreneurial way of doing business was something I wanted to expand. Still, I had bills to pay and needed to be working right away. The fact I had six months to find the right job did not seem as important as finding a good job that paid well as soon as possible. For me, the anxiety of not having job security was the driver of all my actions. I had gone through my first downsizing event, or more clearly stated, job loss. This situation had shaken my confidence and it cut me down a few notches. I doubted the great things I had done with McNeil and at Unilever were not because of my outstanding business skills. Yes, I was concerned I might not find another great job and might have to settle for something much less rewarding than I wanted.

Little did I know how the events of the next few months would impact not only my career but my personal life, were taking shape. About a month into my search, I interviewed for two solid region manager positions. One job I really wanted was with Group Dannon. The job was managing the Florida/Bahamas markets and selling all Dannon consumer items. I went deep into the process but eventually lost out to a young lady with less experience but who was bilingual. I never really took into consideration how my not speaking Spanish limited me in these markets. I was told to stay in touch and they would interview me for the next domestic position available.

The other job was with a large broker in the Tampa market. This company was well established and offered a great package. Somehow, I felt working for a regional company was not as glamorous or weighty as a sales job with a national sales team. I was truly illiterate in my business understanding and this was the second time I had been less than properly excited to be pursued by a solid retail broker operation. The first was with a Jacksonville company, LT Acosta. This fine company would have outstanding success beyond the Winn Dixie and Publix grocery markets and developed into Acosta Sales. They would soon become one of the most well-known and successful retail support companies in the country. I had turned the Acosta owner down flat four years earlier and never really considered the great opportunity he was offering. As I have said many times, my understanding of the real business world was surface and undeveloped. Still, with those mistakes, I had been blessed and maybe very lucky. I had worked for elite companies in these first twelve years of my career. It wasn't until much later I saw how fortunate I had been.

A few weeks later, I had my first contact with the best company you have never heard about. I met a man who would teach and motivate me to be more than a sales manager. As I will detail in the next chapter, I was about to find the best job, the best work experience of my career.

During that time, I would also find a lifelong partner. Wendy, like my old boss at Avondale Mills, would accept none of my excuses for one minute. I met my wife of twenty-seven years at Outer Circle and this meeting allowed us to share life experiences we could never have imagined. We eventually moved to Chicago and enjoyed the final and very best years of my time with the company. The fact she had been our owner's executive assistant gave her an understanding of our principled culture from its beginning. This understanding helped the two of us manage the challenges and enjoy the benefits of this fast-paced company and its empowering environment.

Chapter 3

Outer Circle Products, 860 W Evergreen, Chicago, IL

Nearly two months after my initial interview, I joined Chicago based Outer Circle Products, at 860 West Evergreen, near downtown Chicago. The company office was down the street from Cabrini Green. This was one of the most dangerous public housing projects in the country. The place was approximately ten apartment towers, which were around twelve stories high. Cabrini Green was the subject of a 60 Minutes segment on the murder of a young child by other kids living in the project. This story examined the terrible crime of a kid being thrown down an elevator shaft in one of the apartment buildings. Cabrini was a dangerous place and avoided by most everyone. I had Chicago cabbies refuse to drive me directly to my office from O'Hare, since it meant a drive through Cabrini. Despite the proximity to this very dangerous neighborhood, the area became a second home, and the place I learned how to be a better businessperson and manager. I can't come close to remembering the street address of other companies I have worked with, but I doubt I will ever forget 860 West Evergreen, Chicago, Illinois. It was the home of the greatest company you will never know. I don't think I will ever forget this place or the wonderful people I worked with there.

The hiring process I experienced at Outer Circle was unusual for sure. I had my first interview in early January 1992 at the Charlotte airport and gave up on the job after not hearing anything for nearly six weeks. I spoke to my recruiter, and he said they were slow on hiring decisions, so we might hear something later. As usual with the company, this was the situation in my case. I remember the interview clearly. Larry was calm, honest, and professional. He understood the company mission, and was looking for people he could trust, and people who would also commit to their philosophy. I liked him immediately and hoped I would get the offer. He was not a rah-rah guy, and he was not overly friendly during our meeting. He was organized, clear on what he needed, and honest about the careful consideration both he and I needed to make in the final decision. After hearing no feedback from my interview for over a month, he called and asked me to join him and the company owner in Chicago.

My final interview was the first indication of how great this career move would be. Our meeting was a dinner at a downtown Chicago restaurant, Bistro 110. The reason I remember the place so well was the first thing I ate there. They served us an appetizer of roasted garlic which was spread onto fresh baked rolls. It was something I had never seen. Even though I was feeling a bit like a country bumpkin, Tom explained he had never had this delicacy before his first visit there either. There was no atmosphere of, we are high-level superiors and decision makers, but an air of, let's be open and honest with each other and make some decisions. Tom and Larry were relaxed, genuine, and made me feel like I was already a member of their team. They explained I would be the third member of the sales force and would take over a market with little existing sales volume, but a huge target customer list. I would be responsible for the Southwest, Southeast and New England Markets, which would cover fifteen states. They questioned me on how I felt about traveling a minimum of three weeks per month. Since my most recent position comprised the Southwest, Southeast and Mid-Atlantic markets, I had no concern about the travel schedule or work load. I had already been working in an undeveloped business segment with Unilever by selling food items, the Ragu brands, to a non-foods class of trade. I had experience with the drug chains, mass merchants, club stores, and independents in those markets. This region manager position was like what I had been doing for the past two plus years.

By this time, I had already reached the million-miler status with Delta airlines and was accustomed to nearly one hundred hotel night stays per year. I didn't know I would surpass the three million miler level in the next few years and continue the hotel stay rate. Even with this schedule, the amount of travel did not bother me. When I explained the details of my last sales job, I added the fact they would hire someone who knew how to travel, manage time properly, and would target and add new accounts. I must have been convincing since before dinner ended, we agreed I would join the company in two weeks.

When I began working for the new company, I was unsure what challenges the transition to a small, entrepreneurial company would bring. My twelve-year sales/sales management experience was with two large corporations. Now I was joining a business with total sales of just over $3.0M annually. I had one other job opportunity in the sales world, but based on the interactions I had with these guys, I joined Outer Circle. The conversations I had with the owner and VP of Sales, who would be my direct manager, had created a curiosity about the company and established confidence in them. I felt they were the most honest and plain-speaking businessmen I had ever met. During our initial dinner meeting, I was told they had plans to create a very different working experience for every member of the company. Both talked about how everyone was expected to do anything they could to move the company ahead. They laughed about not having job descriptions, internal politics and useless, empty slogans that added nothing to the success of the business. Those things alone made me excited and happy to accept the offer and join them.

I spent the first three weeks of my new position in the field with one of the other region managers. Rod was their original sales manager, and also a former J&J employee. Working with this very talented and smart guy was an enormous advantage. There was no training manual and no fluff. Rod was honest about the challenges and clear about the direct management style of the company. The most important thing he did was explain to me that I had responsibility for everything in my markets. There were very few support programs and little to no marketing plan other than the basics. He walked me through the product line over and over and tried to make sure I understood who to contact for sales support and materials I would need. I was not disappointed with the new job, but was surprised at how thin we were in every department. Our time together wasn't so much of a training session as a meet and greet schedule with the few existing customers and the current representative groups handling our brands in my three markets. After those three weeks of getting familiar with the territories, I spent week four in the Chicago headquarters office. Larry took the first day to introduce me to the staff and show me how the operation worked. He walked me through the process of how we designed and sold our new product lines. He worked with Tom on each of our new item designs, and the refresh of our existing items. Then they flew to China to work with our strategic partners in their factories to build our initial soft sewn, insulated product samples. From there, all items were refined, marketing materials were created, and the insulated items were shipped in container loads to

Chicago. We inspected each piece, and assembled the final items at our office, which was also our production facility.

When I joined the company, we sold three soft coolers with plastic liners and two lunch kits. One lunch kit was a soft insulated style, and the other was an injection molded item. We also marketed a full line of injection molded plastic music storage products. This plastic product line was the original product mix Tom used to start the company. He designed the items, hired a molding company to build them and sold to the Premium or Incentive class of trade and music chains. One of those first items was the Arctic Zone plastic lunch kit with an insulated drink container inside. This lunch kit was a kid's item and it was molded into several color combinations and was a non-licensed item for the lunch kit promotional season. Unlicensed, meaning it was a plain box without a kid's character or movie theme license.

It was my understanding that Tom and Larry began working together when the new soft insulated lunch kit was created. It was an innovative, soft sewn item and included the existing plastic insulated drink container inside. I seem to recall Larry had gained promotional placement of the soft sewn lunch kit at Walmart, which gave us a foothold in a promotional segment of their housewares department. From there, the company had expanded by adding two sales managers, and increased the Arctic Zone brand with the creation of the soft insulated coolers with a plastic liner. The liner immediately solved the consumers biggest problem with non-plastic personal coolers by making them leak proof; unless you tipped them over since the zipper was not leak proof.

These two men had a great eye for fashion and colors and worked to understand who made the retail purchase and why. They learned how mothers were the primary buyer for lunch kits and personal coolers along with grandparents. Men made a significant level of buying decisions for the larger personal coolers. I was impressed by their understanding of our markets and the details they discovered while still managing the daily business. Both the lunch kits and coolers were stylish and actually worked. This benefit was a tremendous improvement in the product offerings in this small but developing business segment. The color assortments and materials for each product line were appealing but designed for different end-users. The lunch kit items had bright and vibrant colors with similar packaging style and details. The cooler line had a more subdued and adult appeal color palette to meet more mature tastes. Along with my hiring, the company added a new marketing manager to the business. Andy came from the Rubbermaid company and brought additional creativity and marketing skills. It was obvious we had a solid brand, great leadership, and the financial resources we needed to compete. We had talented people in the field and in our headquarters office with fresh and innovative ideas. I will add more details about the team we created later.

My early experiences in this small company made me realize some important business facts. One of the most critical being how a small company has a short developmental time frame. It is why recruiting, interviewing, and the goal of making no serious hiring mistakes is so important. Mistakes are magnified and people in all departments must be up to full speed almost immediately to be successful. There is usually very little chance for a person to blend in and not stand out if unqualified in small to mid-size companies. This is because the attitude must be to accept almost any challenge. In many small entrepreneurial companies, employees must be not only willing, but eager to tackle new challenges, embrace change and show a genuine passion for their work. I also learned a very important fact about employees in these businesses. The way to create a "do anything needed" mindset is to empower people with a sense of trust. They must trust that their stretch or move outside their expertise or comfort zone will be a positive step for them and the company. This is a straightforward thing to say, but a tough environment to create.

At every other company I worked for, the guiding principle of management was to make sure everyone had the mindset of accountability. If you were not doing things according to your direct manager's interpretation of company procedures and the manager found out, they held you accountable. What this also means is if your manager does not find out, you get away with the misstep, real or imagined. Following procedure is important and required in most situations, but an accountability mentality often kills the desire of an employee to stretch and find a potentially better way. Managers do not need to be cops or detectives constantly looking for any violation, large or small. They should be focused on building a better team and getting important work done. At Outer Circle, I learned this accountability style hinders the ultimate results of the overall company effort. The common management thought of, we need positive results, so let's make sure people are accountable, is a true negative. The mindset of everything you do creates accountability means there are times you might hesitate to attempt something you are not sure of, or take a chance to do something better, even if it is not your assigned job. This environment is not a pro-active or progressive management style.

I am sure there are hundreds, if not thousands, of people who completely disagree with my opinion, and that's just fine with me. At Outer Circle we counted on our competition not "getting it" and continuing to move in slow motion or even move backwards. We had an inside joke about how the most common business environment was like a dinosaur, well past its ability to be effective, and out of place. In our principled environment, we experienced growth by individuals, product lines, marketing research, overall sales volume, and net company profitability.

At Outer Circle, we used the term responsibility instead of accountability. When people take on responsibility for themselves, managers have little to no detective work to accomplish. Holding people accountable is unnecessary when they hold themselves responsible every day. A responsible employee doesn't care if a manager is present or hesitate to take risks and even make mistakes. We were confident each employee who really understood our principles, or as we said, "got it", would be successful by taking on challenges. People were confident they would not be criticized, reprimanded, or subject to dismissal for a failure. With this confidence, our people didn't try things in the dark, in silence, or in secret. They didn't hold back questions or any information from managers in fear of an interrogation or criticism. They also didn't hesitate to ask questions. Our folks took on tough projects and made it known they were leading the work. This visibility of their effort made it easy for people with expertise or knowledge of an issue to go to them and offer help.

An example of what we felt was an outdated management style was the phrase job description. I often heard a negative comment from employees at other companies and this comment was, "That job or task is not in my job description". Every time I hear the statement, it makes me feel sad for them and their employer. Something exists in this situation, which makes an employee use the line as a reason to not do something versus an attempt to get something done. Candidates often asked about job descriptions when we interviewed people at Outer Circle. I usually replied to the job description question as follows, "Your job is to do anything needing to be done and to do it as best you can". When people would come to us from corporate cultures, this line usually just stopped them cold. They would get a strange look, as if they wanted to say, "What the hell is wrong with you? Are you serious or just a little crazy?"

A favorite part of my job at Outer Circle was the interview process. We would sit down and tell people, "It is very important for you to listen to how we describe the company. We need you to relax, get comfortable and be honest with yourself and us about everything we discuss". We wanted to get to the true fit they might be, if hired. I was honest with people and drove home the point about the challenges of our culture and the fact we differed from most any company they had ever seen. I always told them our hiring process was very slow and if they were not right for the job, they would hate being with us. It was an empowering, fun, and a very honest way to deal with someone who was serious enough to take the time to meet with you about joining your company.

We never conducted practice interviews. Since our style was direct, honest and for actual jobs, we really didn't need to practice. If a company can reach this comfort level while interviewing people, it would likely have a positive impact on their success, profitability, and employee retention. Of course, this is against today's HR practice of personality tests, problem-solving riddles, artificial intelligence screening programs and the avoidance of face-to-face interview conversations. I find many human resource practices today dumb, cover your ass focused, and hesitant to take responsibility for a new hire. I also find the excuse, "We are too busy to spend much face-to-face time with candidates", a ridiculous and weak practice. No, I am not an HR specialist, just a manager who has interviewed and hired a large number of employees. I believe too many of these practices do not allow firms to find those great employees who are not obvious or the perfect artificial intelligence review fit. These "gems" can be missed because of some process complication. Few things are more important to the company bottom line than hiring the right person for a job. If one employee or a group of people are charged with the responsibility of hiring, they should do it incredibly well. Each person involved in the hiring process should be able to put their name on the candidate. To us, this meant you were clearly saying the candidate should be hired and putting your name on them was a record of your personal approval. Simply stated, this process worked very well for us. We made a few mistakes, but they were uncommon.

For small, entrepreneurial companies, there is usually no built-in time allowance or profitability to carry a weak link. We made sure this was always our mindset at Outer Circle. Another key factor was how many people cannot accept change, or at least rapid change. One of the most common thoughts and later a simple practice was to "embrace change". Learning to embrace change was one of my strengths, and I quickly discovered change is the only sure thing. I learned to be ready for most every program and every customer to change in a short time.

I still hear people today talking about how things used to be better and how things have changed too much. When I speak to young people in high schools or civic organizations, I encourage them to understand and embrace change. I tell them to listen and take any value they can from their elders' stories of the good old days. We all have heard most of these stories. Many of us older, experienced folks say, "We never had cell phones, the internet, Play Stations or the advantage of a Google search". This is true, but it does not mean it is better. It only means it was different and usually less efficient than today in most situations. Yes, there may be negatives in the modern candidate pool. Young people and many new hires have very different expectations from individual jobs and careers. These things are not a blanket negative, meaning bygone days were better. Ignoring change and failing to embrace it doesn't help anyone. In business, this thinking wastes your time, kills growth, and makes people miserable for no good reason. Damn it, things are always changing, so accept it, embrace it and get something done.

New and often younger employees with fresh thinking arrive and depart constantly in organizations, big and small. Each has a different perspective, which could be vital to the next stage of development for some project, department, or individual. Everyone should think more about new ideas and less about how things used to be. If companies could help people understand how to embrace change and stop worrying about the past, this single step would be a serious positive for everyone. It's not only about profitability, sales volume and growth. It is about a culture believing, no, truly believing, the company is their responsibility.

When a core group of leaders or believers gains a small measure of momentum, there is very little they cannot accomplish. Every tough decision becomes more manageable. This is difficult, not simple, but as I learned for myself, a workable philosophy. The word which embodies this culture is passion. The passion I felt for and also felt from the Outer Circle culture and its members was all-encompassing. It didn't occupy my every thought. This passion allowed me to enjoy down time and enjoy my non-work activities much more than ever before and much more since that time. There are conversations today about a changing workforce and non-traditional needs by this new group of employees. It's called change, and it is manageable. If your company truly embraces change and manages it to your advantage, the differences in the current or potential workforce will not be a hinderance but an opportunity to do things better. When Larry hired me as a member of the Outer Circle sales team, I did not understand any of this thinking.

Everything started with our owner and founder, Tom. He was a brilliant young guy who had studied at the London School of Business near the "Outer Circle". As I understood, his vision was to start a company, get it established, and then implement a set of principles as the key to every daily task and interaction. Like so many creative and innovative people, he had the vision and guts to build a successful and better company environment. Thankfully he put his plan in place and supported it totally with the understanding that everyone would be just as supportive. He partnered with people who could run a successful business and support his unique management philosophy. An outstanding example of that ability was our VP of Sales.

While I worked for him and for a long time after, I felt Larry was always the "benevolent manipulator" in our lives. As I have said many times, he always seemed to move or manipulate me to a place which was good for the company and me. He had an incredible ability to manage distinct personalities in the right direction. Maybe it was because I was totally committed to the program and his leadership, but I really don't care. If this part of my career was a total and complete manipulation, I am very grateful for it. He made me think, work and act like a professional. His leadership was always clear, with a confident, not cocky belief he was on the right track. From the early days of my employment, he wanted me to be creative, develop my plan for each market, and work that plan. An example of this leadership is our first sales meeting, which he held shortly after I joined the company. There were five people in the room, Larry; region managers, Rod and Marty; our new marketing manager, Andy; and me. We met in Larry's suite and sat comfortably and casually around the main room. He opened our first meeting with a welcome to everyone and introduced Andy and me. He then laid out what we would do as a team. He told us we had the right talent in the room to make the company grow, and grow in the right direction. He wanted all of us to commit to the sales plan, and work hard to make this company an enormous success. This was a powerful opening statement for our small team. We had significant experience and talent in the room, and he made it clear that our efforts would be vital in making the company grow, and be successful. I had not been in a company like this previously.

I was impressed by how the VP of Sales, who shortly after this meeting became President of the company, sat down with us, told us he believed in us, and asked us to commit. He did not mention how we would all be accountable for our decisions. He did not tell us how important he was or how smart he was. He simply convinced us he had brought us together, based on our skills, and now we would move ahead to make the company a success. Larry sold us on the plan with simple and straightforward logic and clarity. At the end of the week, we all understood his talent, his style and his absolute belief in what we could accomplish. When we departed this first meeting, we were prepared, confident, and ready to take full responsibility for what needed to get done. I thought of our first meeting often as the company grew and developed into an innovative, profitable and market shaping entity.

I left the initial meeting feeling wanted, informed, and ready to work. However, for the first four months of my career at Outer Circle, I did not sell one box of product. I was zero sales for four months. It is important to understand that we were a promotional business, and we accomplished most of our sales in two three-month selling periods. Still, I was feeling down and felt I should give Larry a call and maybe ask for more help or direction. When I spoke to him, he told me I was contacting the existing customers, meeting with new customers and doing exactly what he wanted me to do. He called those meetings face time and foundation building meetings. He said, "Don't focus on purchase orders right now, just keep doing exactly what you are doing, and we will be successful". I noticed he said, "We will be successful". Not that I would be successful, but that we would be successful. Another big change from what I had experienced in past positions. I experienced success at other companies but there was never a similar connection or concept of my being very important like I felt at Outer Circle. We, and I, found rewarding work and great success for many years.

One other thing about Larry was his ability to put together incredible new product launch presentations. We had a national sales meeting twice per year to reveal our product lines for the back to school and summer seasonal promotional periods. After introducing the product lines, Larry would walk the sale team through a mock presentation. He covered each item in detail, explaining how they met consumer needs and fit into our strategic plan. Then, he updated us on new marketing trends and gave us a basic outline on how to build our individual customer presentations. He was, without doubt, the best sales process instructor I ever knew. He could also carry this skill from the classroom setting to the buying office. He was a smooth and convincing presenter who stayed focused in the face of tough situations.

An example of his calm and controlled manner was a final presentation on our music storage line to Radio Shack. After I had made the presentation to this 7,000 plus retail location customer, I felt we would gain placement. Our buyer gave a strong buying signal by confirming our sales estimates and I tried to close immediately. Then the buyer brought up a new and challenging objection. He did not think our Clik!Case brand name was strong enough for his customer base. After a long pause, he told us what he really needed to negotiate before buying our items. We would need to remove the brand name from the injection molded pieces and create completely new packaging. His marketing team would decide the style and colors for the packaging and we could only tweak those designs.

We had quickly moved into an area of expertise I couldn't address. Without an awkward transition or hesitation, Larry moved the discussion ahead. He mentioned the cost of laser cutting our molds to remove the brand name would be approximately $5,000.00 per mold. Then he added the fact we would be forced to add an entirely separate inventory for what translated into a new product line. As I sat in this meeting, I wondered if I had missed his true intentions. Did he really want to buy the line or was he setting me up for a rejection based on our declining to meet his requirements? When he added the fact every piece of merchandise accepted into the Radio Shack warehouse would not be subject to any returns, I was encouraged again.

This is when Larry showed me an example of strong sales tactics. He asked for a couple of minutes to look at a few calculations, and we sat in total silence for a good three to four minutes. It was like an in-person demonstration of the sales axiom, "Whoever speaks next loses something". Finally, our buyer said, "So what do you think? Are we done here or moving ahead?" Larry put away his calculator and said, "If you can agree to adding six items, and place six pieces per store, we have a deal".

At this point, I was a spectator. My mind raced ahead with my own calculations of the size of our initial order. The unit count would be huge, and some of these items were expensive. With 36 units in 7,200 stores, we were looking at orders for over 250K total units on high margin items. Finally, we agreed to reduce the case pack on one item to two units, and two others to four units. We reached an agreement for just under 140,000 total pieces ordered. We gained five new items instead of six, but they would sell each of the five in all retail locations. The initial order was just over $600K and doubled our total sales for the brand versus the previous year.

As Larry and I walked to our rental car, he turned to me and said, "Today was an important day for our company, congratulations". I was beyond excited, but realized he had closed the deal, not me. One thing I asked was how he calculated the costs for the changes, evaluated those cost against our margins and made decisions on the spot. Larry turned to me and said, "Sidski, (using his common nickname for me), I did every calculation I could imagine last night and had them written in my notes. I just took enough time to make the guy think he had us at a disadvantage during the meeting. He feels like he did his job by putting us on the spot. Now we all feel like we made a good deal". I had never felt more overwhelmed in a business situation than at that moment. This guy was ten steps ahead of me and this was one of his greatest strengths.

I spent the two hours before we met for dinner feeling pretty inadequate and less than prepared. Actually, I felt stupid and was a little embarrassed. My boss could have left everything as it was and celebrated his performance. Instead, he continued to be an excellent manager and motivator. During our second bottle of wine, I explained how inadequate I felt about my own preparations. He cut me off, saying he thought I had done a great job. He told me I had made the sale and he had only worked out the details. I wasn't buying it until Larry became the teacher again. He explained how he had all the company manufacturing, shipping and assembly costs, and I didn't. There was no way I could make the same calculations he had made without this information. Then he said, "You just keep doing exactly what you're doing now. One day you will have all those numbers and then you will make the final decision".

When I dropped him off at DFW airport the next morning, I knew much more about what I didn't know than ever before. His decision to make sure I understood the why and how details of our meeting made me want to do all I could to be better. I didn't just enjoy working with this man, I loved almost every minute.

As the company grew, we added incredibly talented people throughout the organization. We had the right type and number of managers, and now we needed to add depth to our marketing and market research departments. We hired talented, focused and hard-working folks into every internal (Chicago office) department. I not only remember all these people, I respect them and learned from them. They were important to me, and with our culture, we were all comfortable conversing as a family does. We would argue, fight and downright disagree strongly, but we never lost sight of the fact that we all cared and wanted Outer Circle, and each other, to be successful. To better explain our relationships, I would say my colleagues were my work family. Not exactly the same as flesh and blood relatives, but elevated above most other working relationships I had experienced. We grew the company from the small organization I had joined with three sales managers and one marketing manager generating $3.0M in sales to a $120M company with over fifty employees within ten years. The genesis of this growth began in a downtown Chicago hotel meeting room with a group of talented employees.

Tom brought us together for a series of meetings, which included each of our internal departments and the field sales team. He wanted everyone away from the office and away from distractions. Our production team and manufacturing line workers were in the same building, but they would have a separate meeting on this cultural change. Tom felt this group should have separate sessions which would more closely fit their jobs and still mirror the culture created in our meetings. We could not stop all activity and hold meetings, but we could create a two-stage development plan to get everyone into the program. We also kept our receptionist in place to manage inbound calls for everyone and be the control point for any emergencies. I was one of three field sales managers who flew into Chicago for two full days of meetings over three consecutive weeks.

Tom ran these meetings, and we were all given details on how the business culture we created would become the guidelines for our daily behavior and apply to everyone in the company. This included Larry, our VP of Sales, all other managers, and himself. We followed a loose outline he had created and, as a group, reviewed the day-to-day tasks we all executed. After our reviews, we created a term or principle for how we felt we should treat each other and react to each business task. I know it sounds much too simple and a little sketchy. Actually, it was both, and this was the beauty of developing our principles.

To start, he outlined how he felt a company culture should operate. Then we slowly and sometimes painfully reached a "principle" or key word which best described how we should manage ourselves every day. We had flip charts and pages of notes hanging all over this meeting room. We drilled into each department almost every daily task and examined how we could best describe how to do each job better. Our three-week journey resulted in an analysis of our entire business, department by department, and soon established the Outer Circle Products Principles. These would be the ideals and action directing our daily interactions and business strategy. From here, we added details we felt necessary to each principle to cover their impact on how we managed our business from that time forward.

Along with establishing our principles through our own input and agreement, Tom wanted to address another common business practice. He felt strongly about the use of the business term, "Company Mission Statement". Much too often, this was some hokey, often flowery statement, which meant nothing as far as the advancement, treatment or benefit of the employees, and added nothing to business practices. With this in mind, we developed what we called our "Statement of Purpose". This statement became the overall description of the daily operation of the company and described what we planned to do together for our employees and customers. It also described exactly how we would move forward by creating an outline for establishing our specific company culture.

Our statement of purpose was, "We will establish a safe and supportive environment for our team and everyone will support our principled environment and culture. We will produce high-quality products and strive to delight our customers and exceed their expectations". This statement became central to our overall Principled Environment, company culture and business purpose. Today you can open your LinkedIn page and see many authors, consultants and supporters talking about better business practices and treatment of employees. There is nothing wrong with this practice and it adds something to the conversation of change. However, words, slogans and the repeating of sound practices mean nothing without action. Changes have to start at the top and these practices must become actions taken each day.

Each Outer Circle Products, Principle and their supporting guidelines, created by the entire company population, is listed below. Along with the individual principles, we included detailed guiding statements which were fundamental to their practice and the success of every individual principle. These accompanying thoughts and guidelines are specific to our business, its daily operation and our interactions with each other. I will examine each principle in a separate chapter.

Openness
*Facilitating an open exchange of a variety of ideas and thoughts on all subjects.
*Everyone is responsible for anything that needs to be done.
*No one should ever be afraid to ask anyone any question about a work topic.
*Each of us must offer and receive feedback to/from each person in the company, including all company managers.

Respect
*Recognizing each person is important and can add value.
*Being aware of how your actions are affecting others.
*Treating others, the way you want to be treated.
*Dealing with problems at the source immediately and with a positive approach.

Teamwork
*Being dependable and depending on others.
*Having confidence and trust in each other.
*Understanding our common goals and working together to reach them.
*Taking direction and keeping on task every day.

Balance
*Recognizing overall obligations both within and outside the company.
*The company will encourage and support balance. It is up to the individual to make it happen.

Taking Responsibility
*Taking charge and making a difference.

*Taking ownership regardless of the outcome.
* Living up to your end of the bargain.
*Being honest with ourselves and our teammates.

Risk Taking
*The courage to step out of our individual comfort zone.
*Challenging the status quo.

Quality
*Doing the right thing at the right time for the right reasons.
*Always asking how we can do things better.

These seven terms outlined our rules and requirements of behavior. After crafting the individual principles, we made sure we understood their relationships and importance to each other. During this time, we reinforced the need to have everyone supporting our new culture and practicing our principles.

We grouped the seven Principles into three linked circles. The circles represented the dominant themes and overlap of our actual daily tasks. We felt certain individual principles were more vital to one or more of these linked circles. Some principles, like openness and respect, carried equal importance in all areas, while others needed an action principle, like taking responsibility and risk taking. We evaluated our daily work and identified three key areas as the major themes for our activities.

Those areas were: Environment – Attitude – Results.

Environment

*Personal space, individual departments and the overall company.

This definition meant much more than the physical space in our building. It meant the entire Outer Circle world and every action we took as participants in that space. The definition included every employee and department. Without this total inclusion, a major cultural change cannot take place.

Attitude

*Always think about your words, actions and decisions and their impact on everyone else.

This is the beginning of linking these three areas of focus. Our entire environment and everyone in it were required to maintain the requirements of a proper attitude. This included how our words, actions and decisions were received by everyone. Since it is each individual's personal responsibility to keep the principled culture alive, a positive and committed attitude to each of the principles was something we all had to embrace for ourselves and every other member of our company.

Results

*We accomplish great things together with individual and team efforts.

This is another point of linkage for these key areas. Results from the work we do as individuals and teams are important. Like many other people, I thought we could add to our principles list. I always thought focus was a proper principle since it meant honest, dedicated attention to a task or plan. We constantly reviewed this kind of input and concluded additional principles suggestions were adequately covered with what we originally established.

One thing our principles reinforced was the reality of running a business. As I mentioned in the opening, just because you had an idea, recommendation or complaint, it did not mean it applied to the culture. Just as we insisted every employee pass along their ideas and thoughts, we trained our managers to listen to all input. We asked everyone to always say what they felt, as long as they were professional and respectful. We stressed how important it was not to be angry or sulk if your suggestion did not move forward. This took us back to the rule of operating a serious business and following proper business practices.

Tom, Larry and our operations VP, Charlie, often reinforced their commitment to the principles and operated inside the cultural boundaries. They took time to explain how this new and different culture was not a, "do the job anyway you like" situation where everyone just did what they wanted. It was a mentality of getting clear and understandable goals for our company and accepting the final management direction on tactics, strategy and execution. Nothing about our culture conflicted with the idea of sound leadership. This leadership came from those charged with giving direction and making decisions.

We built an elite organization and changed an entire retail category. We expanded sales and distribution of the soft insulated cooler and lunch kit segment far beyond what they were when we began. Our small company dominated the shelves in the top fifty North American retailers. We sold products to most major retailers, including Walmart and Target, and also sold to single store outlets who might make purchases of $1K to $2K per year. The idea was to penetrate the overall retail market and establish ourselves as the category leader and innovator. We would never have a huge TV or even radio marketing program, so we needed to build a grassroots base with consumers.

We did this by solving the biggest problems consumers faced, keeping kid's lunches cool, and offering a stylish recreational cooler which worked. Easier said than done, but something we accomplished through hard work, the innovation I mentioned, and a foundation of loyal retailers. We created and kept alive the best environment, best team, and the very best work climate I ever experienced. Nothing before or after is even close. Why did this happen? Because the employees and the entire management group were on board with a dramatic change in our business culture. These are the same people who made this small organization "the best company you never heard about".

As a part of employee development, we came up with strategies to tap into the individual sales team members and our internal departments' creative abilities. We developed a program called, "The Revolutionary Idea". This was a part of our compensation plan and it asked for an idea considered revolutionary in our business. This plan was open to every employee. My idea was to create a small free sample card for our employees to carry around with them. When we were at a retail location or a social event and we saw someone with a competitive item or one of our own products, we could pass along this card for a free sample from the Arctic Zone Brand. We asked people to fill out a comment section telling us where/why they purchased the item we had noticed. We used this information for our consumer research, as testimonials and for competitor information. My plan was accepted and implemented. We then distributed cards to anyone who wanted to take part. I found this tool to be a great conversation starter when I was working retail locations or as a small gift to my direct accounts staff members.

By completing a great number of focus group sessions, we learned what our customers wanted to change or what they liked about our products. We developed a loyal base of consumers. This step was our grassroots marketing plan, and it created a database of comments and ideas from thousands of consumers. We often received photos of kids using our items, many of which we incorporated into our sales presentations and retail product labeling. Their feedback built an extensive file of information from real customers who freely shared opinions, both good and not so good, which helped us fully develop our product line.

We had ideas and suggestions across all departments and, as usual, the folks who "got it" were excited to stretch themselves to be more creative than ever before. One other great idea was for the internal teams to see actual field work by the sales staff. Like many companies, some departments viewed the sales team as a group of people being paid to travel, stay in nice hotels, and have a good time. Since we were a sales result driven company, Larry wanted everyone to understand what a typical sales trip was like.

We had each internal department team member travel with a sales team member for three to four days and visit as many customers as possible. This meant multiple flights, rental cars and hotels. It also exposed them to multiple check in lines, rental car van rides, hotel rooms for one night, then packing and moving to the next city. Our internal partners experienced terrible traffic, flight delays and hotel arrivals long past normal restaurant hours. They helped carry sample bags into conference rooms and set up our product lines. They saw good buyers and bad buyers, great meetings and less than great meetings. These trips were not "milk runs" but actual field sales trips to real customers, which the entire company depended on to be a success. I had three trips with internal folks, and each of these people saw the sales department in a new light afterward. Most told me they would never be able or willing to do this kind of travel and deal with the personalities we encountered every day.

On one three-day trip to Dallas, our accounting manager and a relatively new marketing team member joined me for several sales calls and retail store checks. We had a productive and informative trip and enjoyed learning more about each other's jobs. After breakfast the last day of the trip, it was pouring rain, so I brought our Hertz T-bird around to the side door of the Marriott, near our rooms. I pulled up and saw my colleagues standing near the door under an awning. They were waiting for the rain to slacken before rushing to the car with their bags. Suddenly, a guy came out the door and ran toward my car. He was shielding his face from the rain and ran to the passenger side, opened the door, and sat down. I am sure the moment was more hilarious to me since I was there. When he turned to me, expecting someone different, the look on this man's face was beyond description. He was shocked and couldn't find anything to say, so I offered, "Wrong car, I guess"? He never said a single word. He only stepped out and ran back to the same door and returned inside. The three of us laughed about this goofy mistake for months.

This small nugget from my travel days was crazy, but not as bad as the night a Marriott front desk gave me a key to an occupied room. I opened the door, stepped inside and immediately noticed a lady's dress and stockings lying on the bed. About the same time, I realized the shower was running. I slowly and quietly backed out and almost ran down the hall to the elevator. Can you imagine the disaster this could have been? The lady would have been frightened out of her mind, and I might have been arrested. I had a free room for the night and a complimentary bump in rewards status after several conversations with the hotel manager and a call from the corporate customer service office.

The field sales team also learned more about what happened with internal departments with each customer commitment, and how our programs affected their work. We learned what it took to build the order, ship it accurately and on time, then get paid. We were being included in the total picture of how our company worked and what we could do to make the entire operation better. I heard these words from Larry frequently, "You are not just a sales guy in this company. You must understand the impact your programs have on our internal departments. It is not a real order until it gets built, packaged, shipped, and we get paid for the goods"! Then, he added something I had never thought of before. He said, "We are in the early stages of development. Every promotion you build needs to sell through the retail stores. If we do this often enough, we might gain basic, everyday product placement on store shelves." This philosophy was in place during our humble beginning and we kept this line of thinking going as we grew and became a much larger company.

When Outer Circle Products entered the market, Igloo, Coleman and Thermos plastic products dominated the lunch and cooler business. A small company had marketed a soft cooler item, which was not heat sealed or well insulated. This meant the ice melted and eventually turned the stitching holding it together into mush. Those products failed quickly, and consumers realized they did not work. I particularly remember being at a trade show in Atlanta a few months after I had sold a combined lunch kit and insulated cooler program into The Sports Authority retail chain. My buyer came to our booth and told me about a conversation he had with one of our competitors. We had taken shelf space away from the company producing the inferior line of insulated items. My program had taken away much of their shelf space and the change upset them. Their VP of sales told my buyer he would regret the move to the Arctic Zone brand, as they did not believe we could be successful. My buyer let me know that he planned to mention at his next meeting with these guys how we had sold approximately four times the volume he had planned for our brand in less than six months. He said, "I will ask them who regrets my decision and this conversation now".

As we grew, we completed a lot of one-on-one consumer research. We did surveys and product tests with actual people in shopping malls, at retail stores, and in elementary schools with kids. We would meet with school administrators and tell them about our company and what we wanted to accomplish. We promised to give at least one item to each kid we spoke with during the surveys. We set up rows of tables with our items and most of our competitors' items. A class of kids from each targeted grade level would walk through this area and examine all the product offerings. We asked each to pick out their favorite item. After this review and our note taking, we allowed each kid to keep his favorite piece, or pick out a new one to keep as a reward for participating. This step was one of the best product testimonies and development projects I ever experienced.

We definitely colored outside the lines. Taking our research to the parents buying our goods and the kids using them often gave us insights which led to product innovations. The marketing team also interviewed other members of our team and asked them to describe how they or their kids used our products. We wanted to make sure every employee not only had the opportunity, but felt the need to contribute their ideas to our overall company's growth and development. Since most of the people working there understood, or "got it", we spent many hours reviewing and working on program ideas from our own team. Many of us asked for input from our own children on how they used our products and what item was their favorite, and why.

During my career, I have managed salespeople, customer service departments, administrative staff, brokers and outside sales representatives. Based on what I learned at my first two positions and Outer Circle, I grew personally and developed a managerial style which supported my team and the company. I could show total confidence in decisions, and this was a major benefit. Normally, knowledge, effort and commitment to a plan fully supported by management supports this confidence. When I have had the positive feeling my decisions were the very best for everyone involved, I could be successful in almost any circumstance.

My first exposure to our key managers' belief in and support of our principles came at a sales meeting. A portion of my field team was the Special Markets or Promotional segment. I managed our "promotional markets" salesperson. She took care of a relatively small segment of our business. It was a low profit, high labor business as her customers wanted custom and screen-printed items. During our meeting, our marketing manager gave an update on our latest marketing plans and consumer research results. Larry, now the company president, was sitting at our "U" shaped table and was occasionally typing on his laptop as he worked on his next presentation. When our marketing team member finished her presentation, my sales manager raised her hand. This surprised me, as she was a quiet, low-key member of our team. She said, "Isn't it against our principles for Larry to be working on his laptop instead of listening to the marketing update? Isn't that disrespectful"? My former big company experience flooded back into my mind and I thought, damn, this will not be good. To his credit, Larry stood and told our group he had no excuse. He had not even realized he was doing this and was happy she had called him on it. He had been disrespectful and he apologized to the presenting marketing manager and to all of us. He meant every word as far as I could see. We were all proud of this team member for her courage and support of the principles. With this one event, many of us began to believe Tom, Larry and our entire management team were serious about this major cultural change. I don't remember ever seeing anyone working on other material while someone made a group presentation at our sales meetings.

We had many challenges with the new culture. There were people in the company who just could not accept this style and constantly tried to tear it down. A few people just pretended to "get it" and tried to get by. Most everyone listening to their negativity challenged their attitude. This meant that we lost some good people, but what we gained was a replacement who believed in and supported our culture. One particular and unusual meeting with our owner stands out to me still. We had hired an outside person to become our new National Sales Manager and directly manage the sales team. This guy was from a strict corporate culture and really struggled with our "Principled Environment". Tom had questioned the hire, but felt it was Larry's decision and his responsibility to educate and bring this new guy up to speed on our culture.

This particular afternoon, Tom was discussing a few things with our HR director Stacey. As I walked by the office, I waved to them to say hello, and Tom asked me to join them. I had known Tom for several years by then, and we had an excellent personal and professional relationship. He was honest and blunt with me, and I responded the same. I thought he wanted to know something about our customers or my sales team, but he had other thoughts. He told me directly he wanted me to take a leadership role in making sure my boss, our new sales manager, was reminded of every principle and company culture mistake he made. He explained how he understood I reported to this guy, and he was sure I understood the respect needed to do this properly. He felt I could work for the guy and still challenge him at every cultural mistake to bring him up to speed quickly.

This was a tremendous challenge, and it caused many problems with my new manager. However, Tom was correct, and every conflict was worth the effort. I felt an obligation to support the culture first and manage my working relationship with this new member of our team separately. What Tom really did was empower me and everyone else to point out, respectfully, every cultural mistake made by every new employee. This new sales manager was struggling to embrace our culture and frequently bullied people by being the boss. Tom hated this style because it was coming from a person in a position of power and one who had an enormous influence on many people. Sadly, this guy never got it, and could never understand why employees didn't just respect his title. He resented being questioned and pressed on our company culture and environment. He got a little better, but never truly believed in our principled culture. During his tenure, this problem made our jobs as a sales team more difficult, but in a strange, positive way kept us all aware of the core meaning of the principles. Also, this showed me how tough this culture was to manage, and how important it was to be supported by leadership who fully believed in our principles. He made enough changes to remain with us, but his early rejection and complaints about our culture hurt his credibility and effectiveness.

Our principles were much more than words. They were created, implemented and followed until they became a road map for our daily activities and supported a culture of positive interaction and change. I always believed "environment" was a critically important part of our culture. This was the basic step in gaining an understanding of how to not only set your own goals, but to be a part of a team having common goals. A set of solid principles gives the company, individuals and teams a chance to move both the company and people toward a common end. This is not a simple task, but as I have said often, it proved to be the single best working experience of my career.

My experience and the development of our principles were truly a significant part of my growth as a manager. Things I learned and took to heart from this company stayed with me long after my time there ended. I hope a successful culture like ours could be developed with other companies. The changes a business will experience because of the recent pandemic might be an opportunity to create similar internal work environments and expand positive guidelines for increased work from home positions. There is no doubt the changes we all faced with working from home or in a limited presence at a central office gave us an opening to review how we go about our business and its environment. Perhaps a look at a principled business culture could create a positive change for everyone. My hope is the creation of principles and culture similar to what we developed and supported together, can be duplicated or perhaps adapted to fit other companies. My belief is the way we treated everyone could be a great asset to any business and lead to more personal growth for their staff.

After I worked at Outer Circle for over ten years, the company was sold. An earlier plan to merge our business with the Coleman Company fell through. The original plan was to add our brands to the existing Coleman plastic coolers and continue as a separate division. When this merger failed, the owner made the choice to sell the business to an investment firm. I remember feeling little upset with this idea as most of us felt ownership had created a substantial business and had been open and honest about the future. I had no equity position in the company and this is from my failure to ask for it. I sincerely believe I could have had a minor share if I had made my case and asked to be included. Our ownership group had shown us for years how we needed to be responsible for our own plans. For whatever reason, I hesitated and missed the opportunity. To this day, I have nothing but great feelings about how I was treated from my first day to the day we sold the company.

The toughest year of my career was staying with the company after the sale and watching an inept group of managers from the investment group destroy our business and culture. Even though they had claimed to support our methods, this false narrative went away quickly after the sale. These guys had no clue what had built our business and did not care to listen to any suggestions. They dismantled our team, our customer relationships, and, finally, our business. There was a constant attempt to gut the product quality, grab as much volume and profit as possible, and sell the company again. Their failure to understand how our business segment operated doomed the company. Finally, they fired anyone who had been a part of the previous management team and I found myself out of a job. It is important to understand these facts. The buyers of our business had the right to do as they pleased with the company. Still, the fact their investment resulted in an enormous loss when they dumped the brand gave me a genuine sense of satisfaction.

Within a week of my leaving the new Outer Circle, I received a call from our former company owner and I joined him in launching a new promotional products company. After a year of effort and thousands of dollars spent, including my salary, we agreed to close the business. I have always felt this was my true equity share in the original Outer Circle Products. Tom gave me a great opportunity, protected my income and thus my family as we tried very hard to start the new business. This was the strongest example of loyalty and commitment to an employee relationship I ever experienced, and I will be forever grateful.

I moved back into the insulated products business with the company who purchased the Outer Circle brands from this business killing investment group about five years later. This Canadian company had been one of our major competitors during my time at Outer Circle, and we loved kicking their asses. They had picked up the lunch kit and cooler brands after the investment group sold out. I do not know how much the original investment group paid for the initial purchase, but I was told by my new company president it was a surprisingly low number. While it might sound petty or vindictive, I can only hope they lost every cent of their investment. They had the opportunity to support the culture and continue to grow the people and brand. They made a choice not to do this, and they chose poorly. No investment group deserved this fate more.

The Canadian company had merged the Arctic Zone brands with their items and did a great job of marketing the combined product lines. I enjoyed the position, the work, and the success. I did not enjoy the constant negativity about business in the United States by the company management. This company management never seemed to mind taking approximately ninety percent of its total sales from the United States markets, but constantly disparaged our country as arrogant, lazy and having dumb luck. Even though I hated this return to a dominating, autocratic and profit first business environment, I smiled and kept my mouth shut. I enjoyed the work away from the Toronto office, and I didn't care how wrong or limiting this negative attitude was since I chose not to play the game. This business was totally opposite of the culture I had experienced at Outer Circle. However, I failed to follow one of the most important principles in this situation. I did not fully embrace the changes that came to my career. That was my failure and my responsibility.

I worked for this company for five years and made almost all my sales goals year after year. After leading the company in sales growth and new account volume, they gave me a separation package and told me the sales team was contracting. This was a tough thing, but it was business, and I had to accept the outcome.

The sales world was once again suffering from another financial crisis in 2010. Sales management jobs were scarce, and it took me a full two years to find another position. Don't misunderstand my feelings about this situation. Life and careers can be tough. I had full responsibility for my career and I already knew life was not fair. Being better prepared to meet this challenge fell to me and I didn't manage it well. I learned from that experience and tried to better manage my career. I had a few good work experiences and a few less than great experiences. However, as I look back on my career, I know how lucky I have been and how blessed I was to work in at least one brilliant company. The lessons and values I took away from my time at Outer Circle Products in Chicago have served me well. My understanding of business, management style and even my personal life have benefitted from those wonderful days in a principled environment.

In the next seven chapters, I will examine each of the principles the Outer Circle Products employees designated as the terms and rules we would use each day. We wanted these terms, our list of principles, to create an environment that would make each of us more respectful, more responsible and perhaps more productive. I will also examine the guidelines we attached to each of the principles that spoke directly to our daily jobs, our communications, and our overall business.

Chapter 4

The Principle of Openness

*Facilitating an open exchange of a variety of
    ideas and thoughts on all subjects.
*Everyone is responsible for anything that
    needs to be done.
*No one should ever be afraid to ask anyone
    any question about a work topic.
*Each of us must offer and receive feedback
    to/from each person in the company, including
    all company managers.

During the early days of forming our Principles, we didn't feel they needed to be ranked in order of importance except for the first and second principle. We decided openness was the foundation of all our interactions and the second, respect, was required to assure each act of open communication was done properly. The principles of openness and respect assured a free flow of communication in the right tone for everyone in our company.

The openness principle would guide people in understanding the benefit and need for open and respectful communications in daily work situations. This principle would help everyone accept direction, feedback and conversation about their tasks and make sure any conflict was handled properly. It would also assure proper communications between employees, managers and supervisors. From this beginning point of respectful, open conversations, we would establish how to manage all our conversations. This first, basic step was hard, and early on we struggled with it, and sometimes fell back into established norms. Still, as a group, we worked on getting this principle set in place and having it become the way we communicated.

This did not mean we didn't have conflicts or disagreements. We had the same number of each before we changed anything about our culture. What we learned was to avoid being nasty, political and disingenuous in any conflict. Everyone learned to accept words showing disagreement, dislike, different points of view and suggested changes since they were given with due respect. No, it was not perfect and yes, many of us failed to do this properly. To my knowledge, we did not allow violations of these two principles to go unchallenged. Failures with these principles were often messy, and it took time to recover from our stumbles. However, each failure seemed to make us more aware of the rules and helped us try to avoid getting things wrong in future conversations.

Why was this principle considered the most important? Because it was the key to unlock the correct behavior when speaking and hearing. Open communication drove us to practice our understanding of other principles and furthered the growth of our principled environment. By avoiding insincere exchanges, we made the act of being political, or avoiding the actual issue too difficult to continue. Everyone was exposed to questions on all topics, plans, and views. It became very difficult to play the game of agreeing with one person and bitching to another. The insincere words of being political or gossiping always seemed to come full circle, and the result was worse than being honest. Without an all-encompassing requirement to support the principle of openness, everyone would fall back into previously learned methods and our momentum would be slowed. It was critical and expected of every employee to understand and embrace this different but important method of communicating.

If we examine the four areas of focus in the openness principle, we can qualify the impact on each employee and department. We wanted to add practical guidelines to break this principle down and examine how it impacted our work exchanges with each other and our managers. We had to learn how feedback, even when it conflicted with your idea or perception, was meant to be positive. An immediate need to avoid being sensitive or thin-skinned to feedback was a priority. Everyone had to become better listeners and converse on a new and improved level. This step wasn't easy and a hard change for some of us. The most common statement we shared to support openness and all our principles was the mentality to "embrace change". You could not use the essence of any principle to say nasty or critical things and then claim to only be practicing openness. People doing this were seen as manipulative users of a selective part of the changing culture. These actions were negative, selfish and done without an understanding of what we were trying to change and improve. Making these mistakes didn't help your cause, it only identified you as a person unwilling or incapable of embracing change.

What was encouraging to those of us who believed in our principles was the push back and challenges to these poor attitudes and reactions from a majority of our employees. Most of our workforce embraced the benefits of a respectful, open flow of communications, and we gained traction right away.

Here are the additional specific guidelines we attached to the openness principle.

*Facilitate an open exchange and a variety of ideas and thoughts on all subjects.

This step sounds simple, but it deals with the biggest problem of changing a culture. It means not only supporting, but requiring, an open, honest conversation by everyone on all subjects. Think about your past work environments and insert this idea. Anyone in the company could and should have professional, direct, and, importantly, honest conversations on any plans, ideas, or topics. How often has this happened in your career? Most of us would answer seldom, if ever.

Now imagine a principled environment where everyone is expected to be open about their thoughts on every plan, operation and decision impacting your role. By remembering the simple rule of always being respectful, you could raise any question, add any point you felt relevant and expect an open, honest and professional answer.

Most people find this type of exchange somewhat intimidating and uncomfortable. When you grow in confidence about the results of your openness and the reactions from your colleagues and managers, the process moves forward. Common everyday activities and daily conversations become easier. Our confidence to stretch ourselves and communicate better on major issues or projects increased. Making sure your team members did not experience a "gotcha moment" with openness brought more and more issues to the surface. This atmosphere drew more people into conversations and led to reasonable discussions of the details and tactics under consideration. The idea of being open and respectful, with the goal of doing things better or at least understanding your business plans, encourages healthy exchanges and development of people and departments.

Again, openness does not mean you can say anything you want in any manner. It means everyone should approach difficult situations to have a respectful conversation. This principle requires everyone to be proactive. Each person must get beyond any initial discomfort and speak up when you feel the need to add something. Some of us were not sure how to object, disagree or simply question everyday issues in the proper way. The example of one of my sales team members speaking up in a meeting is a splendid example of taking a risk and sharing a perspective. The example shows how, in our principled environment, an action was questioned because it seemed against the spirit of the principle of respect. The comment was respectful, professional, and accurate. It showed how to follow the openness principle and by raising a fair question.

*Everyone is responsible for anything that needs to be done.

This second guideline to the openness principle is specifically directed at eliminating the idea of a task not being part of a specific job description. It means exactly what is says. Every person should be open to doing anything needing to be done. If the kitchen trash should be emptied, the first person to notice it should take care of it. That potential first person could be the owner, the VP of Sales, the Senior Marketing Manager, or any other employee in the company. If the trade show display is not packed and it needs to go out, anyone available should help complete the task. If the marketing team needs materials assembled for an upcoming sales meeting, and time is short, anyone available should join the task and see it completed. This does not mean abandoning your specific work task to put out any fire breaking out. It means if you are available to help, you jump in and do everything you can to finish the task. Forget the job description excuse, and if you can provide help, get to it.

Some areas of need are more subtle but highly important. We often asked members of another department or team to join sales strategy conversations and planning meetings. It was crucial for people to join those conversations when asked. If you felt you could offer value to a team, we expected you to approach the group and ask to be included. For example, in our early days, we were primarily a promotional company. We sold lunch kits for back-to-school promotions and cooler items for Spring/Summer promotions. As we tried to take retail space during these promotional periods, many accounts asked for concessions. We treated price as a separate issue and dealt with those conversations based on our specific profit margin goals and requirements.

As we grew and added more customers, we saw an increase in direct account requests for exceptions to our standard business terms. One common request was a specific color assortment for individual customers. As a sales guy, I felt this request was simple and easy to support. I soon learned from our VP of Operations how complicated this task made his team's daily work. If we created a single-color case pack for a specific customer, this item had to have a separate UPC code, inventory slot and a specific work order for the production team to complete. Then he explained how a non-standard order created a potential shortage in the overall building of our assorted case pack. If we used twice as much blue for a large sporting goods customer's special assortment, we could be short on blue items for the normal case mix. The other issue is you can become a custom order company and surrender the benefit of your marketing research on what colors sell and how many of each color should go in a 6 pack or a 12-pack case.

As you might expect, Charlie, our VP of Operations, wanted to have a single-color shipping unit in a single case pack to make his department as efficient as possible. However, he understood that type of plan was only possible in the perfect world and didn't exist in our business. When he became involved in our sales planning and sales meetings, the entire sales team gained insight on what requests made order fulfillment and inventory balance difficult. We learned the value of minimizing custom orders, unless they were a true strategic value, and managed our business to keep the operations department's order fulfillment on track. This understanding supported our sales team's need to ship all orders complete and on time.

Many small companies are sales revenue driven and mainly focused on actions which increase purchase orders, revenue and profits. In those situations, management is less likely to be concerned with culture and environment. They may want a good work environment, but in difficult times, culture is much less important than profits. It is risky to put culture on the same level as revenue and profits. What we learned is that the right culture, driven by a principled environment, helped us increase revenue and profits. If you have an environment where everyone can question the decision of simple things like case packs and order building, your company can become more efficient. Understanding the impact your decisions have on other departments is vital and helps make the overall business flow better. Our sales team became invested in operational efficiency and order fulfillment by working to make production tasks easier to complete. Through an examination of the challenges our customer requests placed on other departments, the sales team understood the need to make decisions to lessen these challenges.

The same thing happened when we sent our Chicago headquarters staff on a minimum of three sales trips with our sales team. Everyone joined multiple customer meetings and experienced various markets. We exposed these folks to the pressure our buyers put on us, and our competition's specific concessions. None of those sales calls were easy, but the experience of these meetings gave non-sales employees a firsthand exposure to the field level business environment.

*No one should ever be afraid to ask anyone a question about a work topic.

This last segment of the openness principle is where success and failure of a principled environment lives. If every employee feels secure in asking any question about a work topic, you not only find potential problems early, but you receive input from people who might help resolve problems. The greatest success is when a question leads to a conversation and the discovery of a more efficient way to complete daily tasks.

All too often, questions by employees are handled poorly in a typical business environment. You do not want departments operating in what we called "functional silos", or in isolation. If this happened, they were not following the culture as other departments did. The asking of questions and sharing input is often the best way to find a better way to manage key business decisions. When questions lead to a better way to accomplish a task, it creates a level of confidence with everyone involved. Usually, it is not a simple thing for an employee to ask a serious question about strategy or a process. When people take the risk to ask a question, they are stepping outside their comfort level initially. It is important to support them, answer their questions and honestly evaluate the situation. Under these conditions, nothing is more deflating and diminishing than not being taken seriously. To have those questions answered poorly or ignored sends a definite signal their questions, their concerns, and their interest in being more invested in the business, is unwanted. Very few things destroy morale, commitment, effort and quality more than this failure. Even worse is a reply of, "Because that's how I want it", or, "That's how we do things in this department". Taking the question seriously will add confirmation for the person asking. As we developed this principle, this step became the norm and led to more reflection and evaluation of multiple processes.

Then there is the "gotcha question" from a person trying to test the culture and your commitment. At Outer Circle we had these questions early on from the few people wanting to diminish changes brought about by our culture. The best way to handle this situation is to listen, answer the question honestly and give feedback. The open feedback usually acknowledges the "gotcha question" and asks for the real purpose of the question. At this point, a manager or anyone being asked should directly call out the BS and address it face-to-face. This is where the most basic and common managerial skills are combined with an individual managers' support of the culture. Then it is important to make the cultural support very clear. All good managers should understand how to deal with individual personalities, and this does not change in a principled culture. A good manager knows which employee needs a direct, firm approach and which one needs a supportive boost.

This management skill is required in any business and company environment. We should all know businesses are not like armies. The military perspective is to break down and diminish the individual, and replace individuality with a focus on the unit. This is not a recipe for success in a business, but all too often the environment where employees find themselves.

*Each of us must offer and receive feedback to and from each person in the company, including all company managers.

This segment of the openness principle is fundamental to creating and operating in a principled environment. Everyone must give feedback and everyone must receive feedback in a professional and respectful manner. When we said, including all managers, it meant no level within the company was exempt from every single requirement established by the company principles.

There are no kings, there are no prima donnas, and there are no exceptions to the requirements. This is where you can measure the success or growth of your culture. If the leadership of your company commits to the principled culture, the chance of it growing, and your team managing most daily tasks and interactions better is possible.

If you empower your team by giving them the responsibility of keeping the principled culture alive and well, most will take the challenge and perform better than they have before. Without full and consistent support, your attempt to create a principled culture and better work environment is seen as phony, deceptive, and will soon be absolutely dead.

In summary, the verbal exchanges between every employee and manager have to follow the principle of open, honest, and respectful conversation. This significant change to how everyone speaks to each other is vital to replacing a top-down power flow to a flat line of power shared by everyone. The only distinction is the understanding of who has a final, decision-making level of responsibility. Managers must always accept their responsibility to manage, make decisions, and lead more than rank-and-file employees. A principled culture does not replace or weaken the management level. It changes some management tactics and improves the flow of information. The major change is the increased level of explanation regarding decision making and ending the practice of using authority as a control mechanism.

I can only use my experiences in the Outer Circle culture as a proof source. My level of respect and acceptance in my manager's direction grew and became clearer in the new environment. The same appeared to be true with the direction and decision making I presented to the employees I managed. My perspective of what was going on at every level of our company was consistently positive. Even when I disagreed with an assignment or decision, I felt I had been heard and was given all the information available for the choice made. I felt as if I was elevated instead of feeling other managers were lessened. This work atmosphere was motivating and reassuring.

Chapter 5

The Principle of Respect

*Recognizing each person is important and
 can add value.
*Being aware of how your actions are affecting others.
*Treating others, the way you want to be treated.
*Dealing with problems at the source immediately and
 with a positive approach.

While we felt openness should be the first of our key principles, as it would be the fuel for growing the culture, it was obvious the respect principle had to be the lifeblood of the principled culture. Openness was not more important than respect, but establishing openness as our new style of communicating changed the status quo. It brought the respect principle along as the requirement for every conversation. We wanted everyone to understand the importance of respect and demanded this principle be ingrained in our behavior.

We understood there could be gray areas in some principles we created. There was absolutely no gray area with the respect principle. We placed a special emphasis on being respectful at all times. Respectful, open conversations would be the key to giving feedback, good or not so good, easier to manage. Without a deep commitment to respecting every member of the company, we knew we would fail. If respect toward everyone every day was not assured, our culture was a gimmick and would quickly fade away.

Here are the specific guidelines we attached to the respect principle.

*Recognizing each person is important and can add value.

When we began this major cultural change, we realized we had to embrace and insist on this section of the respect principle as an everyday requirement. Every person in your company is important and must be respected. If you can give them a fair and noticeably great environment, each person has a fair and equal chance to grow. Each employee will have an opportunity to reach their full potential, and with this growth, each also adds value to the business.

When a principled environment grows and develops, some employees discover the cultural changes don't work for them. This doesn't mean they are not important. It does not mean they don't deserve total and consistent respect. This discovery points out they can and should add their value elsewhere. It never means they are bad people. It only identifies the fact they are the wrong fit for the principled culture. Many people left Outer Circle and most found success in other jobs where they were a better fit. Our company and these individuals were winners when this happened.

***Being aware of how your actions are affecting others.**

How many times have you experienced turmoil or seen conflict within different departments of your company? Sales departments can conflict with marketing, and operations might conflict with sales and marketing. Administrative support and customer service departments can struggle to manage their interactions with multiple inter-office teams. One of the primary reasons for our joint work sessions when establishing the company principles was to give a voice to every individual and all departments.

When I arrived at Outer Circle, I had been a successful salesperson and sales manager with Johnson & Johnson and Unilever. I had seen many inter-departmental struggles get nasty and harm the team members and overall daily business activities. As a sales manager, I wanted the internal teams to understand what I needed to get purchase orders and provide the service my customers demanded. I had a distinct bias against what they needed versus what I needed. Many times, I felt marketing, customer service and operations were hindering my ability to increase sales. I took the position they were hindering the sales team's efforts to increase sales and market share growth. I didn't care what they needed, I only cared about what the outside sales team or I needed.

I was completely selfish and uninformed about the less obvious details of the other departments' daily activities. My attitude was the sales department drove the business and everyone should do anything possible to satisfy what my customers demanded. This surface level understanding of how our business worked was weak and damaging. It came from constant direction to be passionate and let no one stop you from getting the business. I felt stepping on a few toes was just how the selling world worked. Not until I joined Outer Circle, did I understand how to work with other departments instead of demanding that they see things my way. I did a better job when I focused on the principled culture instead of my wrong minded thinking. In the business world where sales teams are vital and important, this type of misplaced value is common. Many successful sales organizations feel superior to other company departments. There can be an adversarial relationship with other employees with the mindset that sales are always a priority. When that bias or conflict can be recognized, adjusted or changed it leads to better relationships, and more efficient operations.

One other thing helped me understand and practice the concept of respectful, open communications. I experienced how our operations manager gave immediate, clear feedback. The fact he could have snapped me in half like a dry twig didn't slow down the acceptance of his feedback. Charlie was talented, passionate, and committed to our company and culture. His consistent, respectful, and direct communication with everyone set a great example. By being consistent with feedback, he never left issues open or hanging over a business relationship. He was one of the best people I worked with at any company. His actions were examples of showing how good business practices fit our culture. Charlie managed those solid business practices every day and never steered away from following the principles and supporting our culture. I was at all times confident that we had no open issues between us. I always knew if there was any issue, he was going to address it professionally, respectfully, and immediately.

At Outer Circle, we were tasked with understanding how our business worked from the internal departments out to the field sales team. This understanding helped me create better and more profitable promotional programs, and helped my teams become more efficient with my customers. After arriving in the Chicago office and managing the customer service and sales support teams, I saw the value of working closely with other departments more than ever. I quickly realized how my original "sales guy" mentality had been counterproductive. Even with the changes our culture demanded, I didn't have a full understanding of working closely with our internal teams. I often heard and said to myself, "The office staff doesn't understand what it is like in the field. I am one person representing the company in multiple markets all alone. They don't understand how many advantages they have in areas of support and readily available assets". While parts of this statement were true, being alone in the field setting didn't mean I could be some difficult, selfish, "cowboy" sales manager with separate rules. I soon realized the "they don't understand my job" attitude was BS and harmful. Since I was one of the original sales team members and had moved into the Chicago headquarters office, I tried to pass along many things I learned there to my sales team.

When I arrived in Chicago with the title of National Field Sales Manager, I handled the field sales group, plus our customer support and customer service teams. Near the end of my first day, I met with our company president. Larry had hired me six years earlier, and he wanted to give me an additional task. He directed me to take a different person, or a couple of people, to lunch every day. He wanted me to become a conduit between field sales and the Chicago headquarters staff. My job was to get to know everyone better in a purely social setting. These were not business lunch meetings unless my guests wanted to talk business. Our time together was casual and relaxed. I didn't have a list of topics to present or specific questions for anyone. I was told to take people anywhere they chose for lunch and always pick up the check. It didn't take long for me to become quite popular with my colleagues as word spread about my assignment.

Larry's idea was for me to become an informal link between the field team and our internal staff members. It was fine if no work topics were discussed, or if sensitive topics came up. I was told to keep these conversations private and not report them to anyone, most especially to him. If someone asked for help, I was to follow the guidelines of our principles then use my judgement on possible any follow up. Things I learned from these gatherings were often surprising and occasionally very personal. Sometimes, I felt like a counselor, and at other times, I learned how happy and dedicated people were to our company. Many wanted to talk about what was going on with the sales team and our major customers. These people wanted to understand how their contributions mattered to the final results of sales presentations. I wasn't a cheerleader, but since most of the news during those years was positive, we talked about many success stories. I tried to let everyone, across all our departments, know they could count on me to help. If a sales team issue couldn't be resolved after following the principles guidelines, I was willing to be impartial and reach a good conclusion. Just as I learned a great deal about the sales teams impact on operations, I also learned the same thing from other people and departments. The key to overcoming the isolation of the sales team from everyone else was respectful, accurate communications and teamwork. Since I was a member of many internal teams and the sales team, it was my responsibility to be a coordinator and supporter of each of them.

The respect principle led us to have better face-to-face conversations between the office staff and a member of the field team. I gave the feedback I felt was appropriate and I received positive and negative feedback. My casual, private conversations were intended to help us become a more cohesive team, and I am confident this happened. The field sales group always had conversations amongst themselves and often speculated about things they didn't fully understand. I always felt the insight I gained from a few casual lunches helped us understand individuals and departments better. Our challenge was to limit speculation and simply ask questions. It was true that the sales team was isolated, but each of us had an open door and the obligation to ask clarifying questions. When we got better at these steps, we managed or removed imagined or mistaken perceptions.

I am often reminded of how the sales departments actions impact other departments when I review an event from my early sales days at McNeil. We had a large grocery chain customer in New Jersey experiencing financial difficulties. The account and district manager heavily pressured our finance department to approve a large shipment to the account. The customer had a promotion set up on our best-selling item with support from a chainwide newspaper ad. The sales staff felt this promotion would help them with the customer if they lobbied to have the goods delivered. The credit manager and CFO wanted to stop all shipments because of the customer's weak financial status. The district manager prevailed, and we shipped their order. Two days after the shipment of a full trailer load of Tylenol* 50 count Capsules arrived, the account declared bankruptcy. When we sent a truck to pick up our goods, the trailer load had disappeared. Our goodwill gesture of support failed and wound up as a cash transaction to a diverter. This meant they sold the goods to some businesses at a lower price than normal, hurting area competitors who only purchased from us. This episode helped me understand we had credit managers for an excellent reason.

Another example was how I struggled with one of our first and most loyal Outer Circle customer's financial difficulties. This customer sold our goods in a small retail location and was also a broker, managing several large music storage customers. He had great contacts in the segment and opened the door for us to Radio Shack's 7,200 locations. After months of not being able to pay for several orders we shipped to him, I had to make the tough decision to put his business on credit hold. I was responsible, and it was a delicate issue. My boss had a long-standing business and personal relationship with this customer/broker. After thinking this over, I agreed with the credit department's follow up request to start collection proceeding. I went to Larry to let him know my decision out of respect for his relationship with this individual. His feedback to me was this. He felt bad about the situation, but agreed with, and supported my decision. He said, "It's a tough thing to do, but we are running a business. It is not fair to the company and other customers to make an exception". Then he added the next hard step that my being responsible demanded. He told me to call his friend and explain the situation. He also said to let him know he was available for a conversation to make my point. I'm not sure what I expected from my conversation with Larry, but I should have known his reaction. The support he gave me was another example of being honest, respectful, and responsible. In the end, the conversation was pleasant, the customer understood, and he apologized for not taking care of the problem. A few months later, and after he paid us, he closed the retail business, declared bankruptcy and relocated. Had I not followed good business practices, the payment likely would not have been made, and we would have ended our relationship in a much worse way.

*Treating others, the way you want to be treated.

This basic and fundamental concept of respect at work and everywhere else was always in focus within our culture. The concept of respecting everyone is often talked about and then ignored in times of high stress and pressure. When I, or other team members, made the mistake of forgetting how to treat others, immediate feedback helped drive the importance of this principle. It became the standard for our daily interactions. The principled culture constantly exposed phony convictions or statements at Outer Circle. As this related to me, I learned to be more patient and less frustrated with people who didn't seem to have a sense of urgency. My constant desire for an urgent response was disrespectful in many situations. I allowed my impatience to push too hard and act without the proper level of respect. The lesson I learned was to accept the different responses of others. Even when I was correct about the urgency of a problem, my pushing for action made some situations worse. I received a lot of feedback on this trait during the first few weeks of work in our Chicago office. Again, I learned being right about a particular issue didn't exempt me from following the respect principle in every conversation.

The principles we followed created a combination of demanding behaviors. We had to share our honest opinions while always being respectful. We all had to help everyone reach their goals by solving problems if we had the knowledge and ability. As a group, we were required to understand how the principles were linked to each other. Our culture depended on this company wide level of understanding and practice. The successful transition to this new work environment required every employee to grasp the principles as a whole. You could not cherry pick a specific principle when it fit your personal needs and ignore it when it was uncomfortable. Each of our principles and guidelines were specific and connected to the daily operation of our company.

Everything about the respect principle was clear, expected, and not ignored when the situation was difficult. Each of us had to maintain a respectful attitude and, with that thought as our foundation, follow the entire collection of principles. If we allowed exceptions to this principle, we were only being hypocrites and faking our way through the workday. Respect for everyone was an absolute requirement to make this culture real and keep it alive.

*Dealing with problems at the source immediately and with a positive approach.

At Outer Circle, I learned how detrimental problems not identified or traced back to their true source in a timely manner could become. As our culture grew and became a part of our daily behavior, I saw people dig deep into complicated problems and attempt to solve them. I also learned to embrace the tactic of passing on bad news as soon as possible. If I had a problem with a customer or another department, hesitating to address it only made the problem worse. Getting the problem to the light of day and accepting the normal discomfort most problems create is the only way to resolve them.

There were several situations with my customer service and sales support teams which required me to address conflicts. Some were with customers, some were with other departments, and several were with sales team members. If there was a problem with a customer, I asked our employee for information and tried to figure out what we could do to fix it. Some situations came up because we had made a mistake and we needed to correct it right away. In this situation, it was more complicated since one of the parties was separated from you physically and didn't have any association or obligation to our principles. If the problem was with another department or a sales team member, no matter the issue, both sides understood the obligations.

On one occasion, I received a call from a customer who told me his customer service rep was incompetent, rude and not fit to handle his account. Good business practices required me to acknowledge his problem, listen to his story, and agree to investigate. After a conversation with my team member, I learned this buyer had screamed and cursed her over a shipping error. She had made an order entry mistake, so yes, we were at fault. In the conversation with her customer, she apologized, took responsibility for the mistake and asked how to resolve it. This led to her being berated, insulted, and hung up on. From there, my obligation was to reach out to the buyer and understand his side of the story. After making my apology, I was obligated to have a conversation about the language and threat. When I asked the buyer if these events happened, he admitted losing his temper and using profanity with her. Then he said, "You and that bitch should grow up and not be so sensitive". For one of the few times in my career, I held my tongue and promised to follow up.

After a conversation with my boss, he and I included the sales manager for the account, then contacted the buyer and his manager. Our first step was to speak with the merchandise manager responsible for this buyer. The conversation resulted in an apology to the three of us and a promise to follow up with our buyer. The follow up was handled properly, and we had another conversation, which included our difficult buyer. We did not present ourselves as self-righteous judges and demand the buyer be reprimanded. We acknowledged how business situations can be pressure filled to a point where everyone can lose their temper and react badly. Our goal was to show our employee we did not agree with her being disrespected and to pass this opinion on to the to the account. What we did was apologize again for our error and explain our position on the follow up call results. After our conversations, she and the buyer spoke again and returned to a reasonable and professional relationship. While we knew there was potential to lose this business, we all felt we made the right decision. Afterward, our sales manager did not have any negative feedback or lingering hard feelings with this buyer.

It was clear to me this lack of respect was not a slip of the tongue or a onetime thing. He had no problem disrespecting me or our customer service representative. His behavior was a pattern of bullying and mistreatment of people who he felt couldn't fight back. We took the risk of damaging our relationship and potentially losing their business. We attempted to stand up for what we believed violated being respectful and professional. To be clear, they were not our biggest customer, but they were a significant account for the salesperson managing the market.

In this example, the customer is not always right. I understand emotions can get heated and we can say words in anger over a mistake, but this was beyond reasonable. Our staff was not perfect. We made the mistake and owned it. Our employee was not sensitive, or thin-skinned, she was mistreated. I could have said,

"Sorry, I can't control the people you deal with outside the company". Had I done this, I would have been a coward first and a liar second. My support of the principled culture meant I had to include other people in this issue, plan a next step, and take the risk of losing business. We all decided it was the right step to address the situation and support our employee.

Each time I had to get involved in an internal problem or an issue with the field sales team, I asked if they had addressed the disagreement with the other person. Until either party tried to resolve the problem on their own, it was not time for me to get involved. We felt most issues, if addressed professionally and respectfully, could be resolved without having a manager involved. This meant our employees had to take responsibility and address a few major conflicts. Some were settled quickly and others had to include a manager to resolve the problem.

Having a principled culture doesn't magically make everyone get along well. When I took responsibility for our customer service and sales support teams, we met every Friday morning. To close the meeting, I asked if there were any conflicts needing to be addressed. If someone had an issue, they remained after the meeting and we discussed the problem. Again, I asked if they had spoken to the other party about the issue. If the answer was no, we planned to get together after this step was taken. If it was yes, and problems remained, we talked through the situation and made a plan for a joint call or meeting with the other party. Some meetings were heated, and some were solid learning experiences. Other meetings or calls were cancelled as the two parties talked again and worked things out instead of taking the next step.

While this method usually helped everyone and was most often an obvious demonstration of how our principles worked, it was not foolproof. Some people had problems and held them inside so they did not have the uncomfortable conversation. Usually, this led to more and bigger problems because the initial trouble festered and led to other issues. Our principled culture didn't make everything go well or make everyone happy. As this example shows, you can't work out a solution until you see or are told about a problem. Participation was the key to using the principles to work things out as best you could for everyone.

I learned early in my career how problems only get worse with time. For example, it is never fun to call a buyer and tell him about a problem. Let's say a shipment of goods will arrive late when your buyer has an ad scheduled to support a promotion. If you get this problem into the open right away, the buyer might reschedule or change things to minimize the damage. You will still get the grief, but this is a personal responsibility of managing a business. If you wait, the problem will almost always get worse and the damage will be more significant. By waiting, you are not only disrespecting the customer, you are failing to take responsibility and manage your business properly. The key lesson is to understand how no problem gets better by failing to address it.

We probably had fewer personnel issues than many other businesses, but we had the same business operations problems as any business. Our culture didn't prevent problems, but it helped us resolve many of them quickly. We never had the goal of eliminating failures, mistakes, or any other common business problem. What we did in a consistent and passionate way was to work on them, evaluate their origins and try not to repeat mistakes. When we learned about poor decisions and disappointing levels of success, we viewed those things as effort with less than desired results. Our interests were in the key ingredient of effort. Mistakes made by repeated poor decision making, poor research and not taking responsibility were not acceptable. Those situations were subject to a deeper evaluation by the appropriate manager with an open critique. The remedies offered were shared responsibility for projects, additional supervision, and sometimes more training.

At the proper time, we put lots of energy and effort into examining the causes of our problems. We wanted to have a thorough understanding of what happened and why. Our management team's role was to be available to help anyone solve problems and then understand exactly what had happened. This requirement kept our managers in line with our principled culture and required them to be strong leaders. They had to be involved, examine the details openly and offer clear and respectful feedback to individuals and teams. Sometimes our managers needed to embrace change and critique failures in a new light. Just because we didn't find the right or best results immediately didn't mean new tactics were not the correct problem-solving approach. Staying with the principles guidelines meant no exceptions, no special circumstances, and always required immediate and respectful feedback. After this hard work, managers were tasked with adding measures to prevent or lessen the chance of repeating our mistakes.

If you wanted to be a manager in our company, you gave up the authority of simply being the boss. You were no longer insulated against hard questions or feedback from your teams or individuals. You didn't have a separate set of rules. If anything, you had a tougher job since everyone you managed could question your decisions. The people who fell under your authority could interact with you on any subject without fear, as long as their questions or feedback were respectful.

A few managers could not give up the long-accepted practice of "respect my title" or "respect me because I am the boss". Those people struggled, hated the job and failed. We brought in a new National Sales Manager when my first manager became our president. This guy blatantly refused to adapt and rejected our culture. He once called my room from a hotel bar in Las Vegas after a long day at a trade show. His plan was for the sales team members to go out to dinner together. I told him I was tired, wanted to stay in and get some rest. His exact words to me were, "Get your ass down here right now. Don't challenge me." I had hated this type of pulling rank since my early days at McNeil. I didn't challenge him or anyone else until he spoke to me in that way. I went downstairs, had a drink with the group, and when the boss said, "Let's go", I told him, man to man and face to face, "I mentioned I was tired and I'm staying in tonight. I will see everyone at breakfast". I was part of the team, but I also wanted to be able to decide, as an adult would, about going out after work. I felt my reply was proper and all I needed to say. Later on, my best friend in the company called me from the restaurant and said the boss was upset with me. He recommended I join them. I really can't repeat my exact reply, but it was impassioned and final. I was prepared for more BS the next morning, but soon learned he was sleeping in and joining us later. He pulled me aside at lunchtime and told me I was not a team player and needed to "get in line". Then "the boss" left a day early, telling us to finish our customer meetings, pack the booth, and close the show. He was a boss, but never a leader.

At week's end, I received a call from my former boss, Larry. He wanted input on my conflict with the new manager, and he got it. At the end of our conversation, I asked if we had changed our commitment to the principled culture and if I had been wrong. He said, "No on both questions. I didn't have all the information". Then I asked him if the three of us could meet. Again, he said no, but added, "This is not how we are going to work together. Just give me time to have a conversation on how we talk to each other".

This situation was not good for anyone. I felt disrespected, the new boss felt challenged, and Larry was probably pissed off at both of us. I got a call with a weak apology from the guy about what he described as a misunderstanding. From there, he left me alone, as in ignoring me for the next month, but we moved ahead. Then, there were more conflicts with people in the office and other sales team members. It was a tough time for the company since we had the understanding no person was exempt from the principled culture. We watched a guy in a leadership position ignore the rules and bully anyone who didn't go along with his ideas.

At our next new product launch meeting, he was tasked with holding a training session with the sales team on building effective presentations. No other manager or marketing staff were in the room for the session. We were expecting an hour-long presentation and group conversation on the subject. Our boss handed out a small book and said, "Read this book and write a one-page summary on what you learn. Then, start working on your role play presentations". With much grumbling and irritation, we read the fifty-page pocket guide, then broke into two-person teams, and worked on the presentations we would make in front of the rest of the attendees. As we worked, we noticed the boss drive by in a golf cart and proceed to play golf until everyone met for lunch. The next week, each member of the sales team received a call from Larry telling us a change had been made. We would report to him until we hired a new National Sales Manager. Management above this guy recognized the problem and they acted. This move was tough since a personal relationship with one of our strategic leaders was damaged and perhaps ended with the change.

I damn sure stepped out of my comfort zone by insisting on respectful conversations and direction from this guy. Later on, I learned there were multiple problems with other people in the Chicago office because of his failure to support our culture. What this meant to me was a confirmation of the requirements we had firmly established for everyone in the company. By moving on from this individual, our leadership team showed us how the culture applied to managers and the rank and file.

This dismissal took much too long in my mind, but we eventually corrected the mistake. Our next step was even more frustrating since we made the same mistake again. We again hired someone who was expected to add value and fully commit to our culture. What we hired was an experienced manager from a larger company who had no interest in supporting our culture. The second sales team manager was a poor hire, but he survived by faking support of the culture. This is not a guess on my part. He was my direct manager and, on multiple occasions, let me know he thought the principles were a terrible practice. This was the biggest cultural mistake our company leadership made, and it became a distraction within the company. I never understood the hire since our leadership team was outstanding and committed to the principled culture. Still, we hired the wrong guy in a key leadership position twice. To this day, I don't know why the second guy hired was allowed to fake his way around our cultural guidelines for months. I was still working in my home office, so I didn't experience the initial fallout inside the Chicago office. As I have said many times, we were not perfect and the culture didn't prevent us from making mistakes. The best thing about this situation was how strongly supported our position of, "we have no exceptions to following the principles and supporting our culture". His act was obvious, but the benefit of a developed principled culture kicked in, and almost everyone tried to help him change. Most everyone understood the challenge, and for months, our team worked through his struggle to get on board and support our culture.

He was tasked with selecting a National Field Sales Manager, and he chose me. With no hesitation, I moved to Chicago and agreed to work with him to build a more effective sales department. The two of us tried to work well together. This new National Sales Manager was a hard worker and he publicly told the team that he supported our culture. Still, the change was too much for him. On several occasions, he told me I was more dedicated to the culture than following his direction, and his assessment was absolutely correct.

Finally, I had enough and sat down with him to clear the air. I told him I understood he was my boss, and I was under his direction. I wanted him to know I would support him as long as his plan or actions didn't go against the principled culture. Then I explained how I wanted him to be successful and also wanted him to understand why so many people were in conflict with his methods and management style. To his credit, he listened and remained professional, but he didn't understand why I said any of these things. I told him I was not trying to undermine him, hoping to replace him. I didn't get the job when he was hired, so I knew I was not the choice for the position. We ended with an agreement to disagree on our cultural differences, but would continue trying to work together. After the meeting, he went to the HR department and complained, but was chastised for not being completely open with me about his issues. I learned about this conversation as a direct follow up to his complaint. There was no whispered inside information exchange. I was asked to review our meeting and then asked how it ended. There were no exceptions to the rules established by our principled culture and work environment.

Two weeks later, I had a memorable, unplanned meeting with our business's owner, Tom, who directed me to challenge mistakes made by my manager regarding his support of our culture. He wanted this sales manager to stop faking and honestly support the principles at all times. His exact words were, "Help him get on board with our culture". I respected Tom and understood his concerns with our new manager. I wasn't sure if the complaint to our HR director had been the subject of their meeting. After my twenty-minute conversation, I understood no rank or title came before our culture with Tom. He felt I was committed and strong enough to do what he asked. As I walked out of the office, I understood I had been given a tough but important task.

Later that same day, our HR manager Stacey, stopped by my cubicle and asked how I felt about Tom's request. She assured me it was important and agreed I was in the best position to improve the situation. I asked if my manager's complaint had started this conversation. In her usual style, she said, "Of course not, those conversations are confidential". Then she told me it was important to help this manager recognize how often he was in conflict with our culture. That was it, no pat on the head, or reassurance, only a direct reminder of my obligations.

Over the next few weeks, my manager and I had good conversations and strained conversations. We agreed on many business tactics, but often clashed as he repeatedly told me in private how following our principles was hurting the business. He didn't care if the rank and file had to conform; he wanted to opt-out. The worst thing he continued to do was to pretend to support the culture. He would often say, "I'm following the principles", if he could manipulate a situation by cherry picking some part of our culture to his advantage. He was not a bad guy and was never disrespectful. He was stubborn, had no self-awareness, and was too closed minded to change and grow. Tom never spoke to me about this subject again. I felt he had told me what he expected and left it to me to do all I could to improve the situation.

The frustration with my manager's antics continued with many others and he fell victim to practical jokes since you couldn't talk to him on an equal basis. After relentlessly complaining about how his level of responsibility and rank entitled him to a private office, a small conference room was converted into his workspace. Pushback on his successful lobbying did no good, so he was pranked. His elitism was so resented that a few people came into the building over a weekend, removed the window from his locked office, and filled the room with approximately three feet of Styrofoam shipping peanuts. It was a not-so-subtle message to him on how he should understand we did not have special entitlements for management levels. After a few more attempts to get his attention, he complained to Tom directly. This was the first time Tom was brought into the conversation directly, and it didn't go well. He, Tom and I were the last people in a conference room after a meeting when this exchange took place. I was asked to leave since Tom wanted to offer some feedback in private. Twenty minutes later, I went on my way as their conversation was still going on. My boss and I never discussed the validity of company culture again. There were no more practical jokes, and he seemed to try harder to adapt. Unfortunately, he never understood, and only pretended to be a believer.

Instead of allowing this manager's failure to weaken support of the principles, most everyone rallied around our successful culture and respectfully continued challenging his mistakes directly. These challenges were not done behind his back or passed on to Stacey in HR to handle. People respectfully and openly gave him feedback on his violations of the principles and our overall culture. Most people in our office resented his phony behavior and never gave him a pass. His wrong minded attitude and our constant reminders turned into a positive confirmation of the presence and commitment to our principled culture. Perhaps he had been hired, even with his cultural apathy, to allow our strategic leadership more time to work on the next major change in our company. Behind the scenes, we had been pursuing a merger with the Coleman Company. We were discussing this move with the idea of keeping Outer Circle as a separate division, while adding the Coleman lunch and spring/summer items into our product mix. I believe this partnership would have been a success, but it was never completed.

These two examples were not the only failures by managers. I failed in my new position many times as I moved from a field sales position to leading the team. There were many times I pushed too hard and became impatient. I also used my close relationships with the sales team to gain support of my sales plans and strategy without listening well. The strength and presence of our principled culture was shown to me after my first few months of directing the team. A member of my sales team pulled me aside, gave me examples of my failure, and told me I was not doing a good job. He respectfully and directly gave me feedback with facts, and got my attention. He explained there were times I acted like one of the guys if I needed support, and at other times manipulated other situations. When this less than positive feedback came my way, I listened, apologized and tried to understand my own mistakes. I can tell you I didn't enjoy the lesson, but I understood it was accurate. Once again, the culture was right and its practice made a less than positive situation improve. A member of my own team helped me become a better person and manager by showing his commitment to a culture I felt I completely understood.

The principled culture was not a perfect guide and it did not make anyone happy all the time. It gave me and many others the tools to work through problems and misunderstandings without hard feelings and long-term upset. By reminding all of us there were no experts on the culture, no exceptions to its guidelines, and no prima donnas, it created the best work environment I ever experienced.

Chapter 6

The Principle of Teamwork

*Being dependable and depending on others.
*Having confidence and trust in each other.
*Understanding our common goals
 and working together to reach them.
*Taking direction and keeping on task every day.

There are few things more mishandled and misunderstood than the concept of teamwork. It is always easy to be part of a successful team or think of teamwork when things are going great. It is very different when a deadline is looming, your teammates are a terrible fit, and the workload is not being shared evenly. This is when you can measure the team leader and all the team members. Feeling over matched and a little burned out tests everyone involved. The best example of successful teamwork is when people want to attack and solve a problem or meet a tight deadline and they succeed. It is also a success when the team leader knows everyone worked together, stayed positive and learned something they could apply later.

Teamwork requires trust, sharing the work, and being responsible. Everyone has to understand the common goals and be willing to contribute. There can be no members looking for a free ride with a successful team. Having a strong team leader is the first step in building and maintaining strong, effective teams. It is up to the team leader to focus on the goals, hold effective meetings, and make sure everyone belongs on a given team.

In our principled environment, there was room for individual success, company success, and team success. Each of those accomplishments supported and added momentum to the overall company. Successful teams build leadership depth and increase employee understanding of your business processes and goals. When this type of team momentum is embedded across multiple departments, the culture truly grows. With teamwork as a key principle within our company, it was a common event to celebrate the completion of projects large and small. The closer everyone followed the established principles, like teamwork, the healthier our overall environment became.

Our principles were never a test of loyalty or commitment. They made up a collection of rules focused on behavior, and each was required during meetings and personal interactions. They were not meant to be confining or restrictive toward anyone. People did not walk around on eggshells in fear of a principles error. We had a very loose, very feisty and fun group of people working together to get things done. The reality of our principled environment was how our company supported a creative and fun workplace.

Here are the specific guidelines we attached to the teamwork principle.

***Being dependable and depending on others.**

This is a simple statement and a common description of successful teams. Words mean something, but actions and examples mean much more. I have heard many times that if you want something important done, find the busiest person on the team to lead it. The busy person will always get things done, since this is their normal work approach.

It is always a great thing to be part of a group you can count on to be dependable. That situation inspires most everyone to follow suit and be as dependable as the rest of the team. It doesn't matter if you are leading a group or simply a part of the group when you have the assurance you can depend on everyone to do the right thing and do it well.

Early on, we saw teams forming in various departments with the same one or two people in leadership positions. Those teams were solid enough to add new members without significant experience in some areas and still be successful. The consistent use of our principles as a guide gave most of these teams a chance to be highly successful and noticeable. The reason being, leaders could address shortcomings and give feedback on what they were doing well, along with what was coming up short. As time passed and team members grew more comfortable, we noticed different people taking on significant roles. We witnessed an increasing depth of leadership on several teams and also saw these folks take leadership roles on other important projects. Not everyone made this transition, but many did and made a strong impact on the results of multiple teams.

With a growing level of understanding and support of the overall culture, we felt putting our strongest leaders on problem solving teams in other departments was appropriate. This move not only helped our employees grow, it identified several people who could be counted on to lead, discover innovation and solve a variety of problems arising from our rapid growth. In many situations, the team members from other departments brought a different and fresh perspective to conversations and made positive and valuable contributions. As our depth of leadership grew, it gave us the opportunity to create multi-department teams capable of exploring, understanding, and managing key projects. These teams were also assigned to evaluate and recommend solutions in critical areas, in addition to working on operational problems. We would often times bring in field sales team members to add their perspective to these groups. Combined, they were like a special task force we could focus on problems or major opportunities, and we counted on them to develop recommendations for our management team.

It was a positive experience to watch someone who was shy or lacked confidence, mature and develop skills they felt unsure about. Sometimes they discovered skills they were not aware they had. I have seen people who hated being assigned to a difficult project initially find a strong voice by working on effective and successful teams. One important step for us was to keep the number of team members low and meetings short and efficient. We didn't rush meetings, but we emphasized making sure we followed an agenda, remained focused, and ended them as soon as possible. We didn't set up teams so we could have donut and bagel breakfasts and shoot the breeze together. All our teams reported the status of their goals and accomplishments to a department manager weekly. The only permanent multi-department team we had in place was the production team. Every department sent a representative to this Monday morning meeting, and we covered the agenda and moved on quickly. If you were a member of this group and your area had no issues, you were on your way. People remaining at the meeting's end were looking into real and attention needing situations.

During the ten years I worked at Outer Circle, I felt we were thin in some areas, but not understaffed. I never felt we had anyone with too much free time and too few tasks. I believe this resulted from our culture and attention to the principle of taking responsibility.

***Having confidence and trust in each other.**

This part of the teamwork principle is a natural addition to the dependability tenant. It is a great thing to have confidence in the people surrounding you at work every day. When you add trust to those two situations, you have the formula to accomplish great things. Think about how good it would be to know you could trust and have confidence in your team and every team member. This situation empowers not only the people on the team, but shows everyone how a strong group gets things done. I could see the confidence and performance of our teams grow as our culture and the overall business environment became the norm. Our employees began to believe we were building a substantial business with the benefit of a great work environment.

Another example of our principles in action in the real world took place in a product development meeting with our company's owner. Tom had been working on a molded plastic CD carrying case. Our plan was to sell this storage item into the retail music segment with customers like Blockbuster, Sam Goode, and other chains. We brought the sales team into Chicago and had a meeting away from the office.

Tom had multiple photos of design concepts and a few prototypes of the item. After his pitch, he asked for comments. There was a noticeable failure of enthusiasm for the line and after a long pause, one of our salespeople asked if he really wanted an honest opinion. This sales manager was, in a guarded and awkward way, showing his genuine feelings. What our owner said next was a clear example of his feelings toward the principled culture. He said, "No Rick, I flew the five of you to Chicago from all over the country so you would tell me what a great designer I am." Then with a big smile, he continued with, "Yes, I want to know exactly what you think." With his expectation of getting our open and honest opinions, almost every salesperson said the design, colors and packaging were not right. We told him these items would be difficult to sell to our direct account customers. He paused for what seemed like ten minutes, and they were uncomfortable minutes for us. He finally said, "After hearing your thoughts and looking at the lineup, I think you guys are right. Now, let's talk about what changes you think we need." We spent another two hours working on this product line together. After another six months of development, we launched the items and sold them into our top four music segment customers.

There was much conversation amongst the sales team at dinner and later that night. All of us felt a great sense of confirmation and maybe a little pride in how the conversation had gone with Tom. His reaction was exactly what it should have been. We had no kings and everyone deserved an honest, respectful answer to questions, even the owner.

*Understanding our common goals and working together to reach them.

In my experience, most people work better and are more dedicated to the task at hand when they fully understand and believe in a common goal. We felt our teams gained this type of understanding with the practice of inviting all opinions. If you can have open, honest conversations without fear, you develop confidence and trust in the team's ability to accomplish its goals. When people are asked or simply told to do something without understanding how the task affects the business, the task becomes harder. When you can explain the goal, demonstrate the benefit of accomplishing it, and work with trust and confidence in everyone involved, you have immense power. These things begin with openness and the right people.

We all learned how a single person fighting your principled environment makes every project more difficult, but not impossible. Those who truly don't get it and don't share a belief in your culture are quickly recognized. They are not as valuable as those who want to share your culture, and for a reasonable time, should be asked to get on board. When we began our culture change, there were several people who didn't want to take part. We invited them to embrace change and support our culture. From there, it was critical to move past them if they could not adapt and bring on people who understood and embraced the culture. This staffing change puts a premium on the hiring process. A principled culture is driven by and grows through hiring people who get it, make contributions, and work hard to keep it growing.

Bringing in the right people always puts pressure on your human resource team and managers signing off on new hires. As I mentioned earlier, we asked managers to "put their name on new hires". They would be responsible for the growth and development of the people they recommended. If the employee worked out and became a valuable member of the team, it confirmed your interviewing and hiring practices. If they did not work out, it put a spotlight on the hiring process and identified a need for a review or changes. This obligation was in place for hiring successes and mistakes we made in our staffing process.

Hiring mistakes are expensive for all companies but much more important for small to medium-sized entrepreneurial companies. There are not enough resources to cover for a slow developing or non-compliant hire. Hiring the right person is critical for every business, including a principled company.

*Taking direction and keeping on task every day.

This portion of the teamwork principle goes back to the understanding of business basics. There must be a final decision-making level of management, and this group must have a commitment to a common business plan. As I have said, a principled culture is not a "free for all" style of working. Everyone must take direction, understand and accomplish their primary work tasks as a daily rule. In our principled environment, we took direction from management like every other successful work force. The difference for our company was in how direction was shared. The success of our company depended on running a successful and profitable business. In our company, we found success by supporting our cultural rules which benefitted both the company and employees.

I mentioned in the introduction how I felt my direct manager was a benevolent manipulator. Larry understood how to motivate me to do my best work. There were times he gave distribution and sales challenges I felt were out of reach for my markets. His goal of placing a few of our key items into everyday distribution was one of those challenges. I often asked myself, "How could I convince a buyer to create shelf space for an "in & out" promotional lunch kit or personal cooler?" When I asked for his help, he showed me examples of consistent sales rates with customers carrying our items in basic, everyday placement. He directed me to examine every existing competitive item with this permanent retail placement in my own customer base. His method was to encourage me to use the somewhat limited proof sources or sample size I could find and explain it to my accounts. He wanted me to become the category leader and expert with my customers.

We didn't have Nielsen data for our items, but we could examine customers' monthly sales and ask for details on retail turns. Since most of our sporting goods customers kept a year-round placement on several of our items, we used the results of their class of trade sales data to show potential sales. With every successful test or everyday placement of basic items, we shared the data and added it to our core sales presentation. We set up a "basic distribution" target account list in every region manager's market and worked to gain placement. The focus on this single business growth tactic resulted in outstanding success of point of distribution gains.

Another thing he did was to give me insight into what the company wanted to be in the future. He shared as much as he could on future plans and encouraged me to think about the entire company, not just my individual customers. Some changes we made in our product lines, pricing and business priorities didn't help me manage my individual accounts, but were the best thing for the overall business. This was not uncommon and another real-world business fact. My job was to take our core presentation and customize it to fit my individual accounts. I was given the task of establishing my own goals, and after a review with my manager, move forward or adjust those goals.

I was an intense, driven and passionate sales guy and Larry constantly encouraged me to understand other personalities within our team. He preached patience, tenacity and stepping out of my comfort zone. He told me in one evaluation session, "Your effort and commitment are understood, now work on managing things you don't control". He wanted me to become better at the things I didn't do well as my priority. Then he gave me a list of those things. He moved me into a few projects I hated being part of, then told me he needed my best effort to make them a success. If this truly was manipulation, I am all for it.

To say you have or expect success without solid business practices would expect your business to be a magic act. Nothing is magic about a principled business culture. It takes hard work, discipline and focused attention. There is an element of good timing and good luck in most businesses, but nothing replaces solid business practices. Financing, vision, leadership and excellent management are critical at all times. We showed how our culture fits well with each of those key ingredients by following the principles in our business practices. We saw the benefit of living the principles during our daily work activities. Our measure of success came from improved communications, trust, peer pressure to be a solid performer, and the noticeable benefit of a relaxed and comfortable work environment.

While it might sound like an exaggeration, the great majority of our employees loved their jobs and enjoyed working in our distinct environment. No doubt we had some people remain in the company and pretend to support the principles. No situation is perfect, and no philosophy has full agreement by everyone on all practices. Outer Circle products had enough passionate leaders to overcome dissenters, attempt to convert the less committed, and find a large degree of success.

Chapter 7

The Principle of Balance

*Recognizing overall obligations both within and outside the company.
*The company will encourage and support balance. It is up to the individual to make it happen.

This principle was the most surprising to me as our company and culture grew and developed. In every job I had held, the idea of balance between work and non-working activities never came up. All my working life the focus was on being willing to prioritize work over most every personal issue. My ten-year career at J&J included six relocations. During those years, I built two new homes and never lived a single day in either of them. Just before we completed them, the company transferred me to a new position. They took care of the financial side of both moves, but nothing minimized the personal stress and anxiety we felt by leaving a new home we never moved into for a single night. They gave me the option of taking a new market or a promotion over where my family and I lived. This step was not a punishment, it was an opportunity. Those things were tough, but part of building a successful career.

There was never consideration of not traveling because of a family or kids activity. I flew about forty weeks per year much of my career and this level of travel meant I missed a lot of special things my kids were doing. My office was in my home and this proximity created more than a few late nights working, and many weekends at my desk, trying to manage and grow my business. I didn't blame the company. I understood the job, and I was being paid to do my job well.

After almost thirteen years with J&J and Unilever, my travel schedule at Outer Circle included the southeast, southwest and New England markets. Airplanes, hotels and rental cars were part of most every week so the schedule was the same. The difference was the support I received in maintaining personal balance. When we developed the principled culture and added the "balance" principle, I did not work less, travel less or reduce any of my efforts. This focus directed me to keep life and work in a better overall balance. It was important to the company for me to be in balance with my personal life in order to perform and be at my best while I was working.

When my wife Wendy and I moved to Chicago for my National Field Sales Managers position, my children were still living with their mother in Jacksonville, FL. My Florida sales manager lived in Orlando so even trips to that market didn't give me time with the kids. I went to my manager and asked if I could take a day off when I was in the Florida market and drive to Jacksonville to visit them. Larry was fine with this but added another thought to my plan. He suggested I attempt to schedule field work trips there to end on Thursdays so I could spend my Friday office day in a hotel in Jacksonville. If I wanted to stay the weekend, the company would benefit from a less expensive flight which included a weekend. This plan worked out occasionally, and I was grateful for the flexibility. With this balanced approach, some of my visits only cost me a rental car fee and a few hotel room nights. We all benefitted from the plan and everyone understood exactly what was happening.

The balance principle required the company and the employee to be realistic, honest and fair. We tried very hard to always be more than fair regarding personal time and personal needs of our employees. I received fair treatment on all work and family issues, and I tried to pass the same benefit to my team. Instead of returning to the "accountability" style while working through conflicts, I pushed for personal responsibility and a reasonable following of the balance principle.

These are the specific guidelines we attached to the principle of Balance.

*Recognizing overall obligations both within and outside the company.

While I was in Chicago and responsible for our internal sales administration and customer service teams, I occasionally had a strange task. About once a month I had to go to someone's desk and tell them they could not come into the office over the weekend. This was because of people wanting to work, wanting to be responsible for success, and willing to commit the time to get this accomplished. Understanding when those efforts had become too much lent itself to understanding the principle of balance. We felt it was beneficial to the employees and the company to maintain balance of work and personal life. Being in balance kept people fresh, committed and passionate. It was a key principle which made us a better company.

Since several of the field sales team had the same heavy travel schedule, we were encouraged to focus on keeping a balanced schedule. We understood the demands of our work obligations, but now we were directed to understand and manage our personal obligations. Rearranging a field trip to attend to a family activity was acceptable and expected. I often rescheduled a meeting or field trip with sales team members to manage personal events. Since this principle was a huge benefit, I most likely over communicated on schedule changes I made. I didn't feel guilty, but I wanted a clear understanding of the changes I made. In my experience of managing two internal teams and a field sales group, I never felt the benefits of our culture were misused, except for one exception.

There was one sales manager we brought into the company from a traditional sales force. From the outset, I sensed he felt the principles meant he could do anything he liked, take time off when he felt like it, and manipulate the culture. He was misguided, quickly identified as a "user", and terminated when his behavior began to hurt the people reporting to him and his business. By this time in my career, I had hired and fired a number of people. I had felt bad about every one of the terminations, but understood the step was necessary. When I had reached the point of supporting a termination, I was sure the change was not only the best thing for the company, it was the right thing for the employee. This was the first termination I was anxious and willing to complete. I had seen brazen disrespect and pulling of rank by this manager. I grew very uncomfortable with the manipulative use of a few principles as a personal avoidance of responsibility.

Our second national sales manager had hired this employee. Early on in my relationship with this new manager, I was careful to record issues and problems he created. I felt my direct feedback was being ignored and a separate conversation with my new boss would be difficult. After approximately six months of struggles, I received a call from our company president. He directed me to book a flight to the west coast and fire this employee. After a brief discussion of my opinion on the move, I mentioned this step would be a problem as my manager would not like the move. Larry let me know the necessary conversation with him had taken place and I needed to get on a flight the next morning. I asked what my explanation for the move should be and he said, "He will understand the change". From there, we moved to planning the trip. The airline ticket for this last-minute flight to Seattle was priced at over $2,00.00. Larry asked me to use frequent flyer points to cover the trip, but insisted on paying me the cost of an advanced ticket price for using my frequent flyer miles. I would have been happy to buy the ticket myself just to make this change, but he explained this was how he wanted to handle the situation. I made the trip and fired the guy the next day. I never understood what had happened beyond my own experiences with this employee. He was not happy, but did not seem terribly surprised. I suspected his struggles to follow the respect principle with a few members of our internal staff had crossed a line.

After our leadership change in the Western Region, I promoted a young man who had reported to the former region manager. I watched this talented, highly respected young man, Bert, fill the leadership void, and move our business forward immediately. He stepped into a huge challenge and handled the regions business with ease. He took over the major accounts in the western markets and quickly produced strong, profitable results. His personal growth and the company's sales gains had very little to do with me. His success came from a commitment to understand his customers, ask for advice from other managers, and put in the time and effort the market demanded.

What the principle of balance really did was allow for flexibility when we faced work versus personal conflicts. It did not mean you could skip work when you wanted, or manipulate the balance principle to get away with not working. It meant a sharp focus on better planning to avoid conflicts, then made allowances when conflicts came up.

When an employee understands responsibility, trust and company goals, these exceptions were never a stomach-churning decision. You didn't have to always disappoint your family or fear adjusting your schedule in a reasonable way. It also meant no one had to sneak away. Everyone explained their conflicts, and the company supported reasonable decisions to maintain work and family balance.

*The company will encourage and support balance. It is up to the individual to make it happen.

The principle of balance shifted the responsibility to maintain work and personal balance where it should always be, back to the employee. Responsible and dedicated employees appreciated this principle and managed it well. The company almost always benefitted from good judgement in this area. Even the folks who were banned from weekend work on a few weekends, learned to accept and embrace the balance principle. They eventually learned this idea made them more productive and efficient.

The balance principle was aimed at preventing burnout and maintaining a fair and reasonable balance of work and personal responsibilities. In the beginning, the chronic over-workers hated the plan. Later on, they understood the importance and benefit of the balance principle more than anyone. This principle, like all the others, was in place to build a supportive and healthy company environment for every employee.

Chapter 8

The Principle of Taking Responsibility

*Taking charge and making a difference.
*Taking ownership regardless of the outcome.
* Living up to your end of the bargain.
*Being honest with ourselves and our teammates.

This principle relates to my earlier statement of the value of responsibility versus accountability. At Outer Circle, we wanted to create an environment where everyone took responsibility for their actions and stood by decisions that might be good or bad. Our goal was to eliminate the negatives associated with accountability which implied being caught or exposed, and have everyone feel the need to be responsible. We always wanted to eliminate the concept of punishment or criticism for mistakes. This did not mean repeated mistakes were ignored or forgiven. It meant you should own your actions and not feel threatened if they were not completely successful. What we learned was how everyone who feels responsible for projects, tasks, tactics and strategy was more engaged and fully committed to their implementation and success. I had a great number of failures at Outer Circle and by feeling responsible for them, I tried harder than ever to make up for my mistakes by getting better.

Everyone was expected to understand and follow our principles, but we knew a few principles would take some time to fully develop. The principle of taking responsibility was a mixed bag of response in the beginning. Since we were a small entrepreneurial company, many employees already had the habit of taking on any challenge. The thought of being responsible for the results already existed with many people. We saw a slower adoption of this principle with a few employees from more traditional, large companies. The long-time habit of being held accountable seemed to slow some of these folks, as they sometimes saw the responsibility principle as too good to be true. In our culture we didn't try to split hairs over any differences in accountability versus responsibility. Our experiences proved the concept of responsibility to be superior.

There were several conversations where new employees expected a harsh review of a mistake or a failed project. It was confirming and motivating to see their unexpected reactions to a positive discussion of these situations. The absence of negativity by avoiding the idea of accountability and the positive discussions of how they could be better if they continued to be responsible were rewarding conversations. These reviews were an investment in how they could get better by continuing to embrace the principle of taking responsibility.

In most cases, these people wanted more discussion, advice and direction on how to be successful. As we broke down the limitation of the traditional management status quo, we all got better at our jobs. As a team, we understood there was a genuine partnership in the development of individual careers and the health of the company. To support this partnership, our managers identified and recognized great effort as often as possible. We tried to pay attention to effort as much as we did successful accomplishments. When individuals or teams have success, it is readily noticed. What we wanted to make sure we also noted was great effort, even if the results were not necessarily successful. This was not some type of participation trophy. It was a serious practice at Outer Circle to always identify hard work.

When I discussed this kind of employee development and our overall company philosophy with friends in traditional businesses, I was again met with great skepticism. Many of them felt this culture was something only a few people might ever experience. We became accustomed to these reactions, but were never concerned with doubters or negative reactions. We knew our culture was hard to understand and accept unless you were there to see it in action and experience its benefits.

Here are the specific guidelines we attached to the Taking Responsibility principle.

***Taking charge and making a difference.**

We often talked with potential new hires about not having traditional job descriptions and the need to be willing to do anything needing to be done. We wanted to eliminate the "That's not in my job description", hesitation or excuse. If you felt you had the answer to a problem, or if your skills could benefit a task, it was your responsibility, at the very minimum, to offer your help. Making a positive difference by taking charge of projects was the standard we wanted every employee to embrace and practice at all times. Everyone was given their job responsibilities and we explained what work was expected. We simply eliminated the box created by a job description.

This was another difficult concept for some people, and an easy change for others. Being able to take charge of a situation takes many forms. Sometimes it meant assuming control from someone, and at other times it meant offering your expertise, support and experience. What we wanted to maintain was the consistent mindset of respectfully offering your help, without hesitation, to anyone.

There were a few times this concept of taking charge led me and others to pushing too hard, or trying to take charge when the step was not called for. When these conflicts came up, we followed the guidelines called for by our culture. Had both parties, teams or departments had a conversation and passed along respectful feedback? Were all efforts made to resolve the problem without taking it to a manager? When both answers were yes, our managers did their job and managed the situation to a resolution. Some resolutions meant a shared change to the plans, and others led to a manager making a choice. These were events just like those in any other company, but handled with open and honest conversations. We learned that when people had the goal to make a positive impact and do what they could to assure a successful outcome, everyone involved benefitted. We never wanted someone to bully their way into a situation and demand their ideas be implemented. No one was exempt from the rules and behaviors called for by the principled culture. We wanted a steady stream of input or help given with a respectful and supportive voice. Our goal was to see people offering their help freely and others accepting help without concerns or reservations. The requirement of being open and respectful had to be in place with everyone involved for this practice to be constant.

With competitive and focused employees, tensions regarding the handing over or sharing of certain responsibilities came up. These situations could be upsetting and were often challenging for everyone. There are times some people don't readily accept help, even if it is offered properly. The most common resistance to help was when an offer was misunderstood as a challenge or attempted takeover. Following the principles was the first step in finding a compromise and getting back on track.

***Taking ownership regardless of the outcome**.

It is always easy to take ownership of ideas, strategies, or projects that work or are successful. It is a very different emotion to take ownership of or responsibility for a failed idea. In every situation, I would rather have someone on my team stretch themselves or take a chance instead of moving away from an idea because it was risky. No, we were not saying take any risk or use poor judgement. We wanted our employees and teams to always use good judgement, plan well, and understand the opportunity. There were several situations where teams failed and had to explain the details to large groups. Getting past the very human reaction of being embarrassed or feeling bad about not reaching a goal or failing was a key to the next step. This was the work of finding out what went wrong, or what was misunderstood. When there was a reasonable critique or examination of these failures, the analysis usually gave us insight and lessons were learned. This is not a phony recollection of how things happened. It is a real and true example of something most of us experienced in our time at Outer Circle. We were a fast-paced and innovative company, so it was very difficult to hide from a tough assignment or project.

From a manager's perspective, I felt anything we could do to support our employees in comfortably taking responsibility for their work was a positive. We wanted everyone to take risks, stretch themselves, and accept responsibility for any outcome. This meant we had to make sure everyone committed to using good business practices. Just as it was with following our other principles, the goal was to make every daily task more manageable. In every situation, we felt our principles did not hinder the idea of using sound practices, but enhanced those actions, and created a better end result.

*Living up to your end of the bargain.

My feelings on this tenant of responsibility were strong and ran deep. I did not feel a high level of confidence in anyone who took advantage of the benefits of our principled culture and didn't fully engage in plans of action. It is easy to enjoy benefits, but much more difficult to be a contributor and share in the tough work of strengthening a changing culture. The great majority of us handled our responsibilities in the right way and tried to make sure our efforts and tactics supported our company principles. The few people who felt they could pretend to support the culture and continue to work as they had elsewhere were never fully engaged. These individuals were constantly getting feedback about their lack of commitment and, before long, they faced a choice. They could join the team or leave the team.

Even though we tried very hard to hire employees who understood the principles and were committed to supporting them, we made mistakes. There were times the initial understanding of the responsibilities required to thrive in our culture were not deep enough for some people to grow and develop. This failure was not only an expensive and time-consuming mistake, it was a terrible experience for the employee. This failure also put a burden on the people around them.

One case was so frustrating for me, it led to a difficult exchange. We hired an experienced guy for our operations department who worked closely with the sales team. He had been hired by our second National Sales Manager, who struggled to understand and live the principles in his work. After listening to the new guy's criticism of another manager, the methods used in his department, and his business ability, I challenged him. I asked if he had taken his complaints to the manager he disagreed with directly. The answer was no, and the excuses used as an explanation caused me to lose confidence in this person. I told him, face to face, to leave me out of his complaints and the conversation until he took the responsibility of addressing them with the manager he doubted. I couldn't answer his questions, and he was creating a problem by tearing down someone's credibility without addressing the problem directly. I had every confidence this situation would get resolved quickly. I was sure he would eventually involve his manager and the two of them would, at some point, go to the other manager and complain. His first question would be, "Why haven't you discussed this with me before now?" From there, a passionate teaching moment on following the principled culture would be given. This is exactly what happened, and it was absolutely unnecessary. What should have been a two-person conversation escalated to a conversation involving the three people in conflict, the company president and owner.

It is easy to bitch and complain, but much harder to step up and respectfully explain your point of view. Trying to undermine a manager with other folks was not only wrong, it was disingenuous and against everything our culture represented. It would have been terribly wrong to go along with someone who was, in reality, opting out of our cultural standards. Our relationship suffered, but the noise being made was too loud to escape notice. I was not privy to any part of the final conversation, which was appropriate. The situation calmed down for a while, but within six months, the unhappy employee left the company. While everyone lost something in the short term, in the end, the principled culture was the winner.

Not every disagreement, problem, or conflict worked out this well. We had partial success, total failure, and many times, complete success when addressing and managing our problems. Our culture was not "rainbows and butterflies" with everyone smiling and happy every day. What we had was a mindset to follow our very different culture and be consistent in our efforts to keep it alive and well. This step caused discussions, disagreements and occasional hard feelings. Keeping the confrontations respectful usually removed extreme reactions or serious anger.

*Being true and honest with ourselves and our teammates.

There is no better judge of success and failure than the person who gives an honest assessment of themselves, and is strong enough to be honest with a teammate. This aspect of the responsibility principle always focused me on the idea and problem of internal politics. It was always important to avoid being political. Were you strong enough to be honest and give respectful feedback to a teammate, or did you tell them everything is good and say something different to someone else? Since the act of being disrespectful meant an immediate conversation with your manager, you had to give the proper feedback to anyone you disagreed with or felt had failed.

I never enjoyed being told I had screwed something up, even when it was true. I had a great relationship with my first boss, Larry, but there were a few occasions I disappointed him and made him very angry. The key factor was how these emotions were managed by the two of us. Like everyone else on his team, when I screwed up, my errors were noted, and I received immediate and honest feedback. No one was exempt from follow-up and most of us don't enjoy getting feedback on our own mistakes. However, the honest and respectful feedback I constantly received on errors, or mistakes in judgement made me a better salesperson, manager and teammate. I felt anyone could tell me most anything, as long as they were respectful. The failed projects I handled made me want to repair them or replace them with a much better result. There was never a situation I remember where I was only chewed out and blamed for any failure. Only once did I disappoint Larry to a point where he couldn't give me immediate feedback. This event was a miserable experience for both of us, but without doubt, my responsibility. Our conversation the next day was tough because of how we parted, but in the end, it was respectful, meaningful and motivating.

Even when I was being evaluated or critiqued, I was shown respect. After every mistake I made, with the one exception I noted above, I was given immediate and respectful feedback. Since we were all busy with important and challenging work, most of us received less than congratulatory feedback at various times. Those unnoticed situations were in balance with operating a growing, for-profit business. These were the times we had to be patient, be satisfied with our personal knowledge of the accomplishment, and move on. Our system and way of doing business followed the principles. We worked to be consistent in the way we handled positive, mediocre, and negative results, and this is exactly how it should have worked.

Honest critique and feedback with the goal of making someone or a program better should always be the primary goal for any company culture. This is one of the toughest challenges our changing culture faced, and we never avoided the hard part of keeping the principled culture alive.

Chapter 9

The Principle of Risk Taking

*The courage to step out of our individual comfort zone.
*Challenging the status quo.

Some people are risk averse and this is a fact of life and business. Sure things, with little chance of failure and easy to manage, are acceptable and desired by most of us. Programs with large payoffs and impactful success are usually not available without some personal or professional risk. I never considered myself to be a big gambler but I was somewhat of a risk taker. These two things are very different in my mind. To me a risk is something you can study, evaluate and often manage with an idea of the results. A gamble was a situation with the potential of a big loss or big gain. I think my ability to take some risks came from being an athlete in my younger days and also from having a few years of business experience.

I would almost always take a risk if I thought the result was better than no action at all. However, just taking a swinging, wild ass guess, was not a comfortable way for me to work or live my personal life. As I spent more time at Outer Circle in our principled culture, I became much better at taking risks. I had a very real confidence in being supported even if the risk I was taking turned into a negative result. This did not mean I was not well planned or cautious, but it did make me less hesitant about certain business decisions with more than a normal risk. The other thing I wanted to do was build up this level of confidence in the people I was managing. I wanted them to know they could make risky decisions without always checking with me. There are situations where a sales person is put on the spot and either makes the call to go forward or is taken out of consideration.

One of the risks I did not take turned out to be a huge business success for a competitor. When my west coast manager Bert and I were working together, he located a new account in Colorado by the name of E-Bags. These folks were a start-up company and wanted to use our large size cooler items in their e-commerce business. They would offer a catalog of items on the internet and ship these goods to the consumer. They did not have any brick-and-mortar locations. Bert visited them and examined their unusual (at the time) business concept and new vendor requirements. They were asking for a bigger discount than was our standard, and we had to agree to accept items not sold or returned by end users. He wanted us to make the concessions and move forward with this new customer, but he knew management approval was needed for the pricing and return exceptions. I remember the conversation we had well, and I also remember being surprised he wanted to add this business as a customer. I made the call to pass on the opportunity as they were facing a deadline for artwork on item listings for their first promotion offering personal coolers.

I think this was the first time I used the line, "If they need an answer today, it is no. If they can give me a few days to study the program, the answer is maybe". The customer could not wait so we missed the first promotional period which ran for six months. Bert had managed the situation well and E-Bags wanted us to make another presentation when the next promotional period was reviewed. I had passed this information on to my manager, and our company President. Both agreed with my decision not to set up E-Bags as a new customer. I don't say this to pass the buck on my decision to say no. I made the call and felt it was absolutely correct. We would be taking too much risk with an exception to our promotional allowance standards, and our return policy for what I felt would be minimal sales volume.

As we planned for the next appointment, we were asked by E-Bags to quote three of our best-selling Arctic Zone soft insulated soft cooler items. They chose our Cooler & More 9-can cooler, our Sport 40-can cooler and our largest item, the Arctic Zone 48-can cooler with a removable hard plastic liner. I was impressed with their knowledge of our brand and product selection for their e-commerce business, but I needed to see the numbers. When we met, they showed us the six-month unit sales on the competitive items they had promoted and the return rates. This recap confirmed to me I had made the right call. I seem to recall they offered three Coleman brand soft coolers in their internet catalog. The unit and dollar sales were small and the return rate was around 15% on all items. My region manager Bert had worked very hard to encourage me to keep an open mind on this company. He wanted us to take part in a 30-day test promotion at the very least. After our meeting I agreed to use our items in the test promotion since I felt we had a superior performing, high-quality product line. In summary, the promotion was mediocre even with a much lower return rate. The E-Bags management team urged us to stick with them since their concept was new and needed time to develop. I was not convinced and declined to move ahead with them. I had no confidence in the concept of offering consumer items for sale via the internet. I have been wrong on many business decisions, but this is no doubt, one of my biggest errors.

It took E-Bags several years to develop, but over time they became a very successful business. Focusing on the luggage segment and adding other consumer goods produced a strong growth trajectory and made them an early leader in the e-commerce world. They were sold to Samsonite in 2017 and continue to be a strong brand name today. What I had thought was a terrible risk turned out to be the early stages of a major shift in consumer buying habits. This is an example of one person with vision taking what he felt was a reasonable risk, and another person, not having a clue about the changes coming to consumer buying. My buddy Bert mentions E-Bags to me every so often just to help me remember my limited business vision on e-commerce.

At Outer Circle we wanted everyone to feel the need to evaluate and measure the risks associated with projects and ideas. With the fact you are responsible for the results of your actions, not accountable, we were comfortable with our teams and employees taking risks. Sometimes our risks blew up, and we suffered a setback. At other times, we failed initially, but the risk eventually led to a solid payoff for the effort and planning. Just as it is in every business, large or small, top down driven or entrepreneurial, successful programs and positive results are necessary. The only things that seem to survive by constantly failing are politics and politicians. Businesses without success fail and disappear. We were not a fairy tale entity. We were a business needing profitability, successful programs and innovative, high-quality products in order to grow. When we saw individuals with the courage to take reasonable risks, we gave them more opportunities to use their judgement. As shown by the example of my failure to recognize the potential of e-commerce, we found another employee with the ability to challenge the status quo and take a risk. What we could have learned from Bert's risk-taking proposal might have helped us develop our own e-commerce business. We can only speculate how positive the idea might have been for the company with a new, untapped business segment and sales strategy along with our existing business.

Here are the specific guidelines we attached to the Taking Responsibility principle.

*The courage to step out of our individual comfort zone.

This is one of the greatest areas of personal development we saw in our years at Outer Circle Products. When you see an individual step up in a situation where they have no comfort, but understand it is the right thing for the business, it is very motivating and a confirmation of your culture. This situation is empowering to them and the manager encouraging them to grow. By taking more reasonable risks many of our employees developed beyond their comfort zone and added to our overall success. We had a group of hard working, committed people in our company and it would have been foolish not to ask for their input. They were the experts in various parts of our operation and instead of relying on management ideas alone, we asked for their ideas and suggestions to change our operation and make it more efficient.

I had a sales manager in New England who gradually accepted the idea of stepping out of his comfort zone. I like to think this personal development was in part from my encouragement, but there were many other factors. The most important of these other factors were his hard work and account knowledge. He was a former athlete and took pride in the results he generated in his market. Like me, he enjoyed the financial and personal rewards of success. He had been a manufacturer's rep for our company in our early years, and I hired him as my first direct sales team member. My New England business had grown to a point where we needed someone located in the market to handle the opportunities I did not see, since I was in and out of the market.

His former job responsibility was a manufacturer representative. In that position, he was caretaker or point of local contact for multiple businesses. Each company would assign their sales managers to work with Rick and make sales presentations. This meant he would allow the account manager of his various product lines to take risks and build the business. He was more of a coordinator or appointment facilitator in his previous work. I am not saying this type of work wasn't a good job, but it was not a position that helped him grow as a sales manager. The reason I was confident enough to hire him as a direct manager was his tenacity, track record of success, and his penetration of the accounts in this market. Rick was a known and respected sales manager in the New England accounts.

When he joined our company, he understood he needed to be a difference maker and not a caretaker. Still, he did not have all the tools or experience as a direct sales manager to drive the business. He combined his competitive nature with his ability to be a risk taker and went to work. Rick began to search for a sales style that worked within our culture and also worked for his direct customers. His challenge was two-fold. He had to learn to be a result driven account manager for a single company and find success within our principled business environment.

For several months he tried to land major new business with little success. I remember having a conversation with him on one of our long drives through Boston traffic about his struggles. He was frustrated and felt he might not be the right guy for our team. I asked him how he broke a hitting slump when he played professional baseball. His answer was, "I kept taking at-bats and swinging at good pitches". It was as if I drew a curtain back and he saw the answer to his own anxiety. The answer was to stay in the lineup and keep swinging because eventually your talent will produce hits. He kept swinging and within a few months landed the largest program we ever placed at a major drug chain in his market. From there, his confidence and success rate kept climbing. There were times he swung and missed badly, but I never had to do much critiquing. He was always his own most stringent critic. He often felt terrible about failures and beat himself up, but within a few days he would come back to me with reasons for the miss and ideas about how to go after the business again.

There were also times he struggled with our culture. Our principles were a new and foreign concept to a long-time independent manufactures representative. As I did, he pushed too hard sometimes and for a while, was considered a loose cannon. Still, he was a winner and a guy who wanted to be the best at his trade. He showed me a great work ethic and constant courage to step out of his comfort zone. Rick was a great example of a young sales manager willing to stretch, take risks, and become very successful.

*Challenging the status quo.

Earlier on I spoke about the common statement, "The good old days", and the idea of "That's how we do things". My belief is there are many things to enjoy and remember from everyone's "good old days". I truly believe many of our past days were good, were simpler, and some were very successful. However, they were not necessarily better, just very different. When we hold on to these times gone by, we are holding fast to the status quo. This thought refuses to look for and embrace differences, and potentially better methods of doing many things.

During my time at Outer Circle, we constantly challenged the status quo. When you are a small company and competing against giant, established companies you cannot grow or survive with the status quo. I would guess the travel and expense budget of our biggest competitor, the Igloo Corporation, was larger than the combined total budgets for our marketing and sales teams. When you are in this type of competitive fight, you don't last long embracing the status quo. You must find new, creative paths to drive your business. You must have people willing to take risks, open new markets and create new products.

At Outer Circle the statement, "Challenging the status quo", was not some catchy slogan. It was how we attacked our jobs, our planning, and our programs every single day. It was how we grew from a $3M business to a $120M business in less than ten years. We had incredibly talented people throughout our company. Some had never been asked or required to offer an innovative or creative thought in other positions. The pace of our business growth required everyone to think about and share their ideas on these things. Most every department come up with some type of innovation during my time there.

An important example of creativity, innovative thinking and challenging the status quo came from a member of my sales support team. It is important to note I managed our customer service/support teams and this great idea never entered my mind.

Just after starting her position as my support person, we had two customer service staff out of work because of illness and a personal emergency. While working through this short staff situation, Robin suggested we cross train the two teams. This very good idea began with a relatively new hire who had recently finished training. At the time all sales managers worked with one specific customer service and one sales support team member. We encouraged these two internal staff members to communicate and understand the basics of both teams since they worked with the same sales manager. We felt this was a good plan and insured solid communications between these departments, the customer, and our sales team.

A few days after my conversation with Robin, we converted her position into a "hybrid" support position as a test. We consolidated the two functions with one person which meant the customer had one contact for administrative and customer service questions, and the sales team had one contact for their needs. About two months into the test, we merged the two departments when we lost a member of both teams through normal turnover. There were no layoffs or terminations, but a major change to our office organization by a consolidation with existing personnel. The new system was a success and an improvement in our overall efficiency and communications. This successful idea shows the benefit of our principled culture. Anyone, including a new hire, could come up with an idea, have their thoughts taken seriously, and see a change take place right away.

The most serious risk I took during my years at Outer Circle also had a very successful result. I hired a young man who was only a few years out of college. He had worked for Bristol-Myers in the HBC (health and beauty care segment) in a small, introductory market. He had either left the company on his own for a better opportunity or had been let go through a consolidation. I immediately noticed his determination and desire to learn. I hired him the next day and he became my second Area Manager, reporting to me directly. Within six months he had become a well-known, and successful member of our sales team. Stewart was dedicated to the culture and often told me he never thought he would work for a company with an environment like ours.

Every sales meeting I attended with him was well planned and executed. He was honest, frank and willing to have tough conversations with difficult buyers. He was a perfect fit for our company and the job. When we spoke during our weekly Friday morning update calls, he was what I called, "totally buttoned up". He constantly met his goals, and asked how to get better. He was a challenge to manage due to his work ethic and dedication. He made me a better manager through trying to keep up with his daily task execution and tremendous growth as a sales person.

Here is an example of his willingness to address difficult situations. During his second week with the company, I brought him to Jacksonville for a two-day training session on our latest laptop upgrade and put him in a nearby Marriott. We had a system set up for our personal laptops to call the office after hours and download sales data. At the end of this training session, I asked him to complete the call and download his market information overnight. He had a problem with making the connection with the hotel requirement of dialing an "8" with outgoing calls. Since we were going to dinner, he set the laptop up to make 99 re-dials in order to connect and get the updates before we met the next morning. He checked out before I arrived and as soon as I sat down, he told me he had made a terrible mistake. His laptop had made the 99 calls on re-dial and each outgoing call added $1.00 to his room charge. He was embarrassed and offered to pay for the calls himself. I was surprised about the number of calls but not shocked by his get this done no matter what attitude. I told him not to worry about the bill but to remind me to contact the IT department before his flight home to solve the problem. I wanted to laugh but knew I couldn't. I understood you could pull back on the reins of a strong horse, but you couldn't make a lazy one run at all. His drive to complete every task right away and do it well was inherent, and one of his biggest strengths.

We laughed about this story for years and as I grew to trust him, I shared a few of my own "runaway train" mistakes. He asked for more and more responsibility and I gave him everything I could to test and teach him. His ability, intelligence and work ethic became known throughout the company during his first year. The only concern I had was how to give him more projects and responsibility since he wanted to remain in Atlanta. He was engaged and planned to live there, long term. I knew we could promote him to my position, but after that step, a relocation was most likely necessary. Soon after our first outside hire for the National Sales Manager job, we learned the guy could not manage the Walmart business. At the next national sales meeting, I was asked about taking the position but I wanted no part of it. I wanted to manage people, not a single account. At the end of the conversation, I was asked if I felt Stewart could take over the Walmart account. At our company and most others, only an experienced manager would be considered for this type of responsibility. There was a risk in recommending a guy with little experience for this important job. Still, I didn't hesitate to challenge the long-standing practice regarding Walmart account management. I was sure he would need additional training and patience, but would be a great choice. Then I was asked if he would move to Chicago for the job and I could not honestly answer the question. This is when I took a big risk in my career. I went to him before the offer was made and let him know what was coming. This was not the proper procedure and I knew it. I did not want him to turn the job down without taking some time and giving it careful consideration. I did not tell him I would be moving to Chicago as the National Field Sales Manager in a couple of months.

After our conversation, he wanted my advice. I told him to ask for a little time, talk it over with his fiancé, and live with their final decision. I also told him it was an incredible opportunity and a huge career benefit to have Walmart management experience. He understood the risk I was taking by giving him this "heads-up" and everything worked out. Since he took our business to levels far beyond our highest expectations, I always felt my risk was reasonable. Twenty years later, I still feel it was the right decision.

There were other efforts to challenge the status quo with minor changes. At my personal evaluation after completing my second year, the sales team was assigned the step of taking at least one outside training or development class. Larry asked us to decide what we wanted to do, but retained final approval of the class. I had always been a very organized person and carried this habit with me throughout my career. However, I didn't know how to teach this skill or its techniques to my sales team. After a brief search I found a class called "Advanced Organizational Skills for Team Development". The course was offered in Dallas over a two-day period. Larry was fine with the time requirement and costs, so I scheduled the next class for I seem to recall $500.00, and flew to Dallas.

During those two days of class I was bored to tears much of the time. There was a lot of reading about organization and discussions on the psychology of what made people more or less organized. However, I did pick up one technique I still use today. The instructor asked us to follow a simple but effective process. She told the class to begin by writing down our most important tasks for the next day at the end of each day. The first step was to write the date on the top of the page and build our to-do list. Then, we should strike through every task as it was completed. If the task needed any additional follow up, or was not completed, we should circle it. The first step the next morning was to transfer the circled or incomplete tasks to the next page, date it and work through that list. She suggested setting aside a specific binder, legal pad or notes file on a laptop for this activity. At first, this sounded like something a ninth-grade teacher might assign their class. In reality, its simplicity was the key to its success. I began this practice at the end of the day and decided to try it for at least thirty days. Now twenty-six years later, I still use this method. Later on, I learned to only review my tasks binder for circled tasks instead of copying them to the next day.

What I found was a clear, easy to locate and orderly way to track my important tasks. After the first thirty days I was also able to see a history of my tasks by date. After six months I had several legal pads, then bound notebooks, with an accurate record of my important activities. This workbook became something I traveled with and it replaced a scattered collection of notes on various papers, presentation binders and other files. I had an easy to find recap of my most important tasks in one central location.

At my next region meeting, I passed this idea on to my team and asked them to commit to a thirty-day test. Some loved the idea and others dropped it as soon as the test period ended. This idea was not a mandate, but a technique that could be used exactly or in some altered style. The biggest benefit to this simple method of organization was its efficiency. I didn't waste any time searching for my notes from field trips or account meetings. Everything was easier to track and keep in focus with one tool. For me, this turned out to be the best $500.00 in company funds I ever spent.

Almost everyone was put in the position of taking risks at Outer Circle. Some risks were big and some were small, but our company growth constantly pushed us to make tough decisions. We were no different from any other fast growing, entrepreneurial company, except for our principled culture which supported us all in many key areas. Encouraging people to take reasonable risks was one of those important areas.

Chapter 10

The Principle of Quality

*Doing the right thing at the right time for the right reasons.
*Always asking how we can do things better.

Early in my career with McNeil and Unilever, I watched these companies work to provide high-quality products to their consumers. Yes, both offered items that were consumed or ingested by end users. That fact put a major focus on quality control and secure production of our products. When I moved to the housewares segment of the consumer products world, I saw major differences in the level of, and commitment to, quality.

Our Arctic Zone items were a new brand attempting to penetrate a market dominated by major competitors. To compete right away, we overbuilt our goods. We used 420 Nylon as the outer material on coolers and lunch kits. It was incredibly durable and resisted tearing, which was a common failure of competitive items. We offered the best soft sewn products in our categories with innovative Arctic Zone items. We also added plastic inserts to several lunch kits and most of our insulated coolers, preventing them from leaking. Those innovations addressed quality immediately, and we secured retail distribution and saw strong consumer take away.

We also worked hard to provide great packaging, color assortments the consumer wanted, and we inspected every item. All our orders were packed and shipped from our facility in Chicago, and this gave us the benefit of touching every item. We entered a category where existing products failed much of the time and as an alternative, we delivered a high quality, fashionable alternative. As the brand grew, our competition imitated our goods and offered similar items at a lower cost. They did this by copying our style and reducing the quality of materials. In response, we innovated and found lower cost materials, which also performed well. We moved away from nylon and used an extruded vinyl material. As an innovator would be expected to do, we solved one problem consumers had identified. The smooth surface on the outer material was much easier to clean than the original mesh surface. Instead of simply trying to compete on price, we examined new materials, tested it with consumers and remained the leader in quality and value. By maintaining performance and improving our package messaging, we continued to grow our retail presence and remained the dominant brand. At the end of the next promotional season, we discovered the new materials performed as well as our initial high-end offerings, and this innovation made us price competitive.

We never marketed our brands, focusing primarily on price. Our sales strategy was to respond to price pressure but maintain our position as a premium, high-quality brand. Our consumer research revealed there was a low-price market, and we responded with a direct import program for certain customers. Other than those special situations, we continued to compete with innovation and high quality instead of price. In our research on pricing, we learned lower income customers were some of our most loyal users. Their position was easy to understand after we completed more focus group research and gathered information. These consumers needed to buy one lunch kit or one cooler item per season. They could not afford to spend more to replace an item that failed. They bought our items based on a realistic quality/value decision instead of price alone.

We also completed an extensive amount of research with our own hourly production workers. Our predominately Hispanic work force explained their long-standing focus on providing quality goods for their children. By being inclusive and working with everyone in our company, we discovered valuable marketing insights within our own building. Instead of missing this value consideration and assuming a premium item would not appeal to lower to middle-income families, we found a new and loyal group of consumers. We didn't talk about "out of the box thinking", we ignored all the boxes and searched for new information.

As major customers like Target and Walmart refused to accept price increases or demanded lower retail pricing, consumer items in multiple categories saw reduced quality. If you can't raise your price, the only way to maintain your margins is to go with lower quality materials in your finished goods. To address this issue, we created specific products for these two dominant retailers. Walmart wanted a custom item not sold at Target, and Target wanted the same exclusivity. We used our creativity and design expertise to meet their demands and still offer a solid, high performance product line. By never focusing on being the cheapest brand, we were compelled to innovate in order to grow our brand presence. We adapted to market demands and maintained our focus on quality and value in our goods. I would offer our rapid sales and market share growth as our biggest proof source, or record of success. The performance and value of our brands moved us from an in and out promotional company to an everyday shelf presence with many of our customers. Those year-round product placements were not a gift. They were earned by generating constant unit sales and profit for our direct accounts.

The best thing we did for our overall business, other than creating a principled environment, was maintaining a constant search for innovation. Our innovation created different and high-performance items that we could offer to meet consumer needs. The other decision we made was to avoid many business segments focused only on low-cost items. We presented our product line to large companies such as Dollar General and Family Dollar, and we developed low-cost items meeting their profit margin requirements. We wanted to understand those large "low price" retailers even if they would never be key customers for the Arctic Zone brands. What we learned from this process was how they developed their own "house brands", and this knowledge helped us with our own small direct import business segment. Creating items for these customers made us refine our own low-cost items and improve our manufacturing process. Having a lower priced, direct import program was a reasonable step for us, but it was not our focus. Our primary business focus was the development and manufacture of high-quality items that performed and sold to the largest consumer segment.

Here are the specific guidelines we applied to the principle of quality.

*Doing the right thing at the right time for the right reasons.

This step meant we had to make marketing, product design and production quality decisions to meet market demands. We never offered items we knew would fail the consumer. We understood our customers and left the low-quality goods to the direct import producers. With this plan, we continued supporting and following our statement of purpose with the overall goal of meeting or exceeding our customers' needs at a great value.

This mentality also applied to our internal decisions. We were comfortable paying for talent and offering a competitive benefits package. The company never pinched pennies when it came to supporting its staff. We spent as needed to make our work space comfortable and secure. We remodeled our Chicago facility into a beautiful, astatically pleasing and efficient work space. Our 200K square foot building had a very cool style and was constantly complimented by our customers when we brought them inside for business reviews and new product launches. You can find a collection of photos of the interior of our Chicago office at: Office-Outer Circle–Jordan Mozer.

We always tried to take our customers off site for sales presentations. To make these meetings productive for the customer, we often catered lunch and valued their time and schedules. Our sales managers "propped" our items to show how consumers used them. We filled various lunch kits with kids and adult lunch items to show capacity, flexibility and performance. We filled coolers with ice the night before to give a visual reference to their performance. Our sales team constantly worked to be real world, honest, and innovative vendors. We decided to use actual consumers' images on most of our product packaging and this resonated with our buyers and end users. We tried to create a true grass roots marketing strategy and connect with people buying our goods.

*Always asking how we can do things better.

We met this challenge in two distinct ways. We conducted lots of consumer research in focus groups and with school-aged children to confirm our designs and color assortment. We interviewed parents and grandparents, who were the key purchase decision makers in the lunch kit segment, to discover what they needed. We held focus groups with construction workers and adult office workers to discover what was needed from our items to meet their needs.

Then we analyzed and shared the data with our retail customers. We created sales material, clearly showing how our items met the needs of their customers. Sometimes, we did research in their stores and shared what their own customers wanted. We worked with them to create merchandising, retail displays, and promotional programs specific to their businesses. We tried to be their key source of reliable information, become category specialists and trusted partners.

We kept the internal focus on how to do every task better. Our work to innovate extended beyond the products we created and sold. We tried to find innovation in all departments and become more efficient in every task. For example, the sales team needed a constant supply of fresh samples for sales presentations and customer meetings. This need put a strain on the four-person sample team in our operations department.

As our customer base grew, the sales team scheduled an increased the number of meetings, and this increase in sales presentation meetings generated a greater sample item need. This increase put pressure on our presentation sample availability and we saw quality and assortment issues. There were many weeks I would present a cooler or lunch kit program to a buyer, pack up the samples and fly to another appointment. If a buyer wanted to hold on to a specific sample, this meant an overnight shipment, or worse, a missing color in the sample set. As you would expect, packing and repacking samples could lead to less than perfect items for the next meeting. Since nothing was more important than the items you were showing your buyers, we needed a solution. We held a meeting with two sales team members and the manager of the sample team. Together, we came up with a pre-packaged sample kit available to the sales staff. This kit could be ordered in advance and shipped by our customer service team to a hotel where meetings took place. This took pressure off the internal sample building team and the sales team. The change allowed us to accommodate the volume needed by the sales force. It also allowed us to agree to last-minute meetings or unplanned sales opportunities. We could order a fresh assortment of customer specific items as needed without forcing the sample team to work overtime or scramble to build a full sample set. Our changes made the entire process better and more efficient for both departments, but more importantly, supplied the right items for our sales meetings.

In this example and many others, our company principles compelled us to work together, respect all departments' needs and embrace change. We could often find solutions to problems and make multiple processes better and more efficient through open, honest, and constant communication. The environment at Outer Circle helped support a free flow of conversation between different departments. The culture our principles supported also made these conversations easier to start and helped us implement changes quickly.

Chapter 11

The Outer Circle Products Shared Areas of Environment/Attitude/Results

After crafting the principles and the supporting guidelines for each one, we focused on the much larger issue of our total working environment. We looked at how our entire company operated daily. This examination led us to put a focus on the bigger picture, which was our shared interactions. We were confident our principles were a great beginning, but we needed to take things one step further. We wanted to be sure we understood how our conversations and different needs were shared. Our dedication to the respect principle always set the tone in our cultural development conversations.

To support our newly established principles, we came up with three linked circles which represented the major themes, behaviors or actions from our daily work. Each of these linked areas was impacted by multiple principles at various times. Some areas were more impacted by what we identified as "actionable principles", but all were positively supported by multiple principles. This made perfect sense as our work spilled into and complimented all shared areas of focus.

We identified these shared areas as: **Environment - Attitude - Results**

Certain individual principles were more central to one or more of the linked areas and had a lesser impact on another. Still, they were all linked in such a way as to have a powerful impact on each other. Our overall environment was shaped and made better by a constant positive, respectful attitude, and those two things had a tremendous impact on our overall company results. Likewise, this environment lent itself to maintaining a focus on living the principles in our work with open interactions and respect as the fundamental requirement for every employee. Our goal was to strive for a proper, shared, and positive attitude as a team. It was never perfect, and we understood this from the beginning. We wanted to create the circumstances and conditions to move us all toward the right attitude. We expected our company to be a better place to work and our team to be happier, motivated, and dedicated to keeping our culture going. We were confident our business results would be more successful within this environment, and all our results would be the product of our attitudes and the positive atmosphere we worked to maintain.

Environment

For us, environment meant more than the layout or design of our central office. While those things were important to the health and comfort of our employees, we felt the environment was an overriding condition encompassing our every action. This linked circle covered everyone and every department, and as we constantly repeated, no one was exempt. We also understood we were a for profit business and would face the same problems as every business. As I have said, our company principles did not replace or remove any sound business practices. It was not magic, was not a trick, and it was not something we halfheartedly supported. Strong, committed leaders and dedicated employees supported and developed our positive environment. Nothing about the successful culture at Outer Circle happened by chance.

Establishing a list of principles means nothing if they do not have the proper road map or guidelines for how you manage all your employees and your business strategy. It was an enormous risk for our company to begin this radical change of behaviors. Our owner knew if this idea failed, it would damage his and our management team's credibility. His faith in the process and the potential benefit to everyone inspired him to take this risk.

I believe we would have continued to be a successful business if we had never created and implemented a principled business culture. However, I don't think we would have been as successful, and I don't think we would have seen the massive personal growth we experienced with this culture in place. I can honestly say I grew professionally and personally in our culture, and much more than I had grown anywhere else. The success, peace of mind, and passion I experienced there were invaluable. I took many of the lessons from our principled culture with me to other positions and companies where nothing like the Outer Circle culture existed. To me, this is the real and true success of our entire philosophy. The principled business culture changed me as a person, businessman, and manager. This is what experience is all about. It is the gaining of knowledge from the events you go through and the lessons you learn while making the trip. We all know you can't buy, teach or fake solid business experiences. Those experiences are the payoff for your effort, attitude and interactions in your career.

personal space, individual departments and the overall company.

Our culture created and supported the idea of personal space in a variety of ways. We had personal space to think, develop, and prepare. There was no "one size fits all" reaction and adaptation to this new and different culture.

The rule of having no individual with an exception to the company principles was the basic first step. Our owner and management team were expected to meet the same requirements and perform the same as every individual employee and department. Each of our principles; Openness, Teamwork, Respect, Taking Responsibility, Balance, Risk Taking, and Quality, had to be present, understood and practiced in every department and situation. Without a consistent dedication to our principles, we were only pretending, and that type of plan is always a loser. Employees can spot a phony or insincere culture or environment a mile away. In my personal experiences, they always resent an attempt to deceive them.

By understanding everyone learns, adapts and develops in different ways, we made the idea of personal space an important part of how we reached our best results.

Attitude

Performance in this area was as varied as the individuals in our company. Not everyone performs the same, thinks the same or even feels the same. Again, a "one size fits all" description of attitude did not exist. Some people were passionate, vocal and outgoing in their daily work tasks and support of the company principles. Others were quietly dedicated and focused. We did not want cheerleaders or noise makers on the principles typically. We wanted everyone to understand the principles, believe in their value and commit to using them as a daily guide.

Some departments or situations called for an outward display of following the principles. Other situations' use of and participation in the principled culture were not as visible. The greatest need was a consistent awareness of how every individual should follow our principles. Again, not if or should the principles be our guide, but the habit of living them without hesitation. We wanted everyone to be open and respectful without an emotional evaluation or hesitation. Our primary goal was to assure we understood, practiced, and conducted ourselves in accordance with our principled culture.

For everyone in the company, the key behaviors related to attitude were openness, respect and taking responsibility. The specific support of all the other principles varied from situation to situation.

*always think about your words, actions and decisions and their impact on everyone else.

This tenant of attitude was our effort to be specific and detailed about daily exchanges. Words, actions and decisions mattered in our company. There were people I absolutely did not like at the company and I assure you there were people who did not like me. Those are simple facts of life and business and were real-world situations. However, the overriding requirement was to show respect no matter what, in all situations.

Our decisions and personal interactions always impacted everyone else in the company. By making sure we kept this fact top of mind, we hoped to avoid any negative practices or statements appearing to target or diminish an individual.

To not be aware of and sensitive to these things would only expose a level of hypocrisy which would make our principled environment and culture unsustainable.

Results

*we accomplish great things together with individual and team efforts.

As a salesperson and then a manager, my results were most always visible and easy to define. This does not mean they were more important than the results of a team member in any other department. The packaging line, reception, sales support, customer service, HR, purchasing, accounting, IT group or quality control employees' actions might not be as visible but are absolutely as important.

As I said earlier, our production line workers had a separate principles review and training session. I did not often work directly with this team but I understood we had low turnover and they were a happy and dedicated hourly work team. With this group our approach was to follow the exact same group of principles and create the same positive culture. Some applications or situations might be different, but the benefits, opportunities and level of respect was an exact match.

We did not allow any special kingdoms, and no area was exempted from the principled culture. No department was superior or higher in importance. We believed every person in our company contributed to our overall success. We didn't just say this as a disingenuous, "we care so much" statement for everyone. We paid attention and identified strength, contributions, and value across our teams and individual employees. Likewise, we did not want any functional silos where a person or department might feel separated or insulated from the principled culture.

The leadership of Outer Circle was not only in the hands of our owner and senior managers but also with every employee. Every person in our organization who followed our culture and supported our wonderful environment was a valuable leader.

Chapter 12

Conclusion

The Outer Circle Products Principles Summary

The principled culture and individual principles reviews presented in this writing are my best effort to provide an accurate review of them. The examples I have added along the way are also real. It is obvious by now that I was a genuine believer in the culture at Outer Circle. It could be said I was such a strong supporter I could have overlooked or ignored some faults with it. This could also be a true fact. However, I don't believe for one second, I missed the overall beauty, benefit and motivation from this different way of looking at a company's internal workings. My personal and professional growth and sense of accomplishment, along with many others, are much too real to be easily dismissed. We created something there worth discussing and investigating. We saw our culture change the lives and careers of many people. This book will most likely not be a money-making venture derived from a real "dream company and job". I wrote the book to remember the best moments of my business career and to mention many of the best people I have ever known. I enjoyed writing about a company which stated loudly and often its most important cultural rule was one of respect. This word is defined as "regard for the feeling, wishes, rights or traditions of others", as I learned from my google definition search. This fits the style of our operation and supported our overall company environment.

This definition made me ask myself, "What is respect in our daily working lives?" Is it a feeling or a personality trait? The first word of the definition seems to be a reasonable answer. Respect is a regard for a list of things other people are due. This is a powerful concept and one that fit our culture well at Outer Circle.

In our world today, respect is not very common and the respect principle would not be at the top of the list for politicians, activists, media members or a great number of citizens. When our small group of coworkers gathered in Chicago to talk about creating a better workplace and company, respect was the first and most important rule. In our company, you could make a costly mistake, you could disagree on a plan or you could simply be a sketchy personality without reprimand. However, if your personality or actions were disrespectful, you were soon looking for a new job. If we had stopped our list with only this single principle, we would have made a splendid choice and been a better company.

We were a great place to work, and we grew into a successful and profitable business. Investment groups are not in the habit of spending millions of dollars to purchase weak or dying companies. The culture I detailed in this book was simple to describe and incredibly difficult to keep alive and well on a daily basis. Every single member of the company had to decide they could commit to every principle and live them, at least while at work. The concept of a principled culture was not a motivational gimmick or a short-term experiment. As I mentioned earlier, if this entire experience was a set-up to make us all work very hard with no intention of making us better, sign me up again. I would love to have the challenge of once again working in a principled culture.

On the first day of this process, Tom set the initial steps in motion and we all went into a downtown Chicago hotel meeting room with no idea about what he was planning. He gave us a brief overview of his thoughts on a basic concept and we began making our plan. He acted as a referee, not the final decision maker in all our conversations. The final words we used as our list of principles came slowly and became final after several changes. The benefit of these conversations was to have everyone either give an opinion, listen to other opinions, agree or disagree, and reach a final definition. It was also a way to have a group conversation about the function and specific work done by every department in our business. One big challenge was to avoid having a "my job or my needs" conversation. He wanted all our conversations to be about more than just our own personal wish list. Tom did not lead us to a final result he had predetermined. We gathered, spoke honestly about what we felt, and agreed on the final structure. Everything we discussed was loosely guided into a big picture or all-encompassing company environment.

I recall having a sense of relief when we finished our list of principles. Then losing that feeling when we learned we had to break all of them apart and establish the "must have" guidelines to make them understood and effective. From there, we spent the same time and effort figuring out the overall environment and the three linked circles impacted by our individual principles. I believe the Statement of Purpose conversation took one full day to complete.

The entire process was exhausting, but as we completed more analysis, we saw the framework for what would become a desirable end result. When we reached the end of the three work sessions, we expected to struggle and fail before we built the mental muscles to follow our own guidelines. The beginning was an enormous challenge. We were in a competitive segment and we had a business to manage. Our work force was a very diverse group of personalities and some of us needed time to change our communication habits. Being on the field sales team in a home office away from the core group added to those challenges. The overall adoption of the new standards and consistent practice of our culture quickly impressed me. Since we communicated often within our sales group, we questioned what was really going on. Let's just say we were late adapters and needed reminding often. I think our boss being called out on a principles violation during a company meeting, and his positive reaction, convinced the sales team the cultural change was real. His reaction was a simple but incredibly strong demonstration of leading by example. His example impacted our entire sales team, and it moved me to a new level of understanding and desire to get on board.

It will be difficult for anyone who was not part of our company to understand how the culture became a living thing for most of us. I hope a few of my former colleagues will read it and recall those wonderful days. I hope they can recall most, if not all, of our principles, but I sincerely hope they remember the results of our efforts. I also hope they have a sense of pride for all we accomplished and feel proud of our individual and company results. We were never the biggest company in our business segment, but we were by far the most dedicated, innovative and driven to succeed bunch in our business category. More importantly, we created an environment that respected and supported everyone in the company.

While it is easier to understand the impact and importance of respect, other individual principles can be more difficult to grasp as vital for a business. Openness or the need for feedback and varied opinions on many issues was vital, but a difficult habit to form. Early on, we fell short on this principle as we hesitated, pushed our opinions too hard, or didn't push back by being open at all. As it is with all companies, leaders took over and led by example with this concept. My friend and early mentor, Rod, served in the Marine Corps and had no problem with openness. I never saw him being disrespectful, but he could be very direct and plain-spoken. I learned to be more open with Larry by witnessing the two of them practice openness. There were a few instances where the length of their exchanges and the tone led to a separate conversation, but not often. I can say I had those same follow-up conversations based on my open feedback with him, as I suspect most sales and marketing team members did. We all learned better methods of giving feedback when we had a different point of view or totally disagreed with someone. All it took was time and practice to support this principle, and our management team gave us the room we needed to learn.

The balance principle was always something outsiders did not easily understand. Managers from other companies with a traditional manager/employee relationship questioned this principle more than any other. I saw many people dismiss the idea of balance out of fear. The old saying, "If you give someone an inch, they will take a mile", was the common excuse. Some of my friends at J&J thought the idea was a joke, or at least a phony concept. They did not believe a manager could ever show any understanding or agree to placing a personal issue over your business needs and obligations. This is logical, since it was not a concept, or practice they had often experienced. Many managers were exposed to the idea that mentioning a conflict with a family event or hesitating to relocate to any market was viewed as a weakness. Those were the feelings and the understanding I had during my time at McNeil. Even when someone had a conflict, or ran into a family issue, there seemed to be a lingering stigma to the event.

The unwritten rule was as a unit manager at J&J, you could, with a valid reason, turn down one offer of a district manager's position. I turned down the Seattle District just after my second child was born. Taking a wife from Jacksonville to Seattle with a newborn and a two-year-old wasn't the right plan for me. The fact that this district was smaller in sales volume and had fewer team members than my unit position made me decide to take the risk and say no. When I met with the regional manager who had offered the position to turn him down, he was understanding and supportive. Still, he warned me how some region managers would see this as a huge negative and might never consider me for their district manager openings. I was comfortable with my choice and the fact that this district closed within a year confirmed my decision.

The anxiety by some managers of our balance idea was likely based on the fear of losing control or not being thought of as a higher-level authority. In reality, our culture created a strong level of respect and a desire to repay or balance the experience of time off or flexibility (balance) from most all employees. We overcame the need to be an authority and managed our teams by trusting them. If there was a way to examine the unwritten ledger in these situations, I am convinced the company came out ahead. I don't recall many situations where I, after the fact, questioned allowing balance of work and personal life with a member of my team. The balance principle was an asset to Outer Circle, not a liability.

When I looked back on the individual principles as I started this book, it was obvious how they worked together and complimented each other. Still, several were what I would call "stand-alone" concepts or guidelines. Respect, Openness and Balance all seemed to work well in concert with the other principles, but also were of singular importance alone. These three principals were foundational, and in some ways opened a path for the others to link and support development of the overall culture.

The principle of teamwork was focused on accomplishing great things together. The respect and openness principles strongly supported teamwork activities since they were our foundational principles. The balance principle was applicable here as well, since it supported an even workload and shared responsibilities. All our teams were important since we created them for specific, necessary tasks and projects. Besides getting things done, our teams helped identify talent and powerful leaders. They gave people opportunities to show their strengths and stand out, or they gave people a path to learn and grow. We had departmental teams and multi-department teams at various times address a variety of issues. One of our greatest strengths was the impact our talented teams had on creating efficiency, finding innovation, and solving problems.

Taking responsibility was another of the "actionable" principles impacting our everyday interactions and work. If you look at how we wanted our company to operate, we wanted all employees, either individually or as a team, to be willing to take responsibility. This commitment gave us a group of workers willing to get things done and be comfortable with the results, good or less than good. What this idea really meant was we expected and supported people being personally responsible for everything they did. Our experience was that when people were comfortable taking personal responsibility without fear of criticism, they were more often successful and accomplished their goals more often.

Risk taking was also a contributing factor to our overall growth and success because it motivated people and encouraged them to step out of their comfort zone. If you remember, it was our practice to manage people with the idea of responsibility, not accountability. The removal of criticism and a negative evaluation of actions taken removed the hesitation to avoid risks. We took some risks which were costly and backfired completely. Others helped us find fast paced and profitable growth. We became a team of aggressive, passionate and successful individuals who worked without the burden of accountability, separate rules for certain people and bullying managers. What we created was the best company you never heard about.

All these things I have mentioned combined to give employees the power to be hugely successful while being overall content with our work environment. Whether you call these things processes, attitudes, guidelines or principles, they led Outer Circle Products to experience great results.

Just like every other for-profit company, we were in business to make money, but much more important than this measure was a powerful environment as a final result. We wanted to execute our work tasks in the best way possible for all employees, managers and the owner of the company. We were never phony, never interested in tricking people to work harder and always supporting the culture we had created.

My repeated statement remains the same. My move to this small, entrepreneurial company, Outer Circle Products, was the best time of my working life. This is where I learned how to do business and also learned how to lead with a positive style to better impact the business and people around me. Our business growth and success led to the sale of the company to a private equity group. I was happy for the Outer Circle owners and wished them the very best. After ten great years of success, it was time for them to sell the business. They were open and honest with us about this plan and I feel most of us understood their decision. There was no reason for Tom, Larry, Charlie and other equity owners not to take this step and make a profit on their investments of time and money in this business. Still, with the change of ownership, I felt terribly lost. I had no equity in the company, so I remained behind for about a year after the sale. Working with the new management team was one of the most difficult years of my career. I disliked and disagreed with their business practices from the minute they became involved with us.

After the sale of Outer Circle Products, our culture was abandoned and replaced with a "get as much money as possible from customers as quickly as you can" philosophy. I conflicted with their style and practices and this conflict grew with every termination of a long time Outer Circle employee. No, I did not embrace change, and I was absolutely wrong in my actions. At the time, this did not matter and I wanted them to know they misunderstood our business, but even more, how little they understood our great team. It is not difficult to guess how this situation worked out. My passion for our culture did not fit their plan, and they let me go. I knew it was time to move on, and I had to find another job. I loved Outer Circle, and loved my impact on the business and teammates. It was a wonderful organization and environment, and working there was one of the most significant things in my life.

I was very fortunate to have our owner and founder, Tom, offer me a position with a new company he had established. I worked with Tom and another former Outer Circle employee who had been our molding process engineer. Tom maintained our pay levels, and we set out to develop a new promotional item company, based on the original Outer Circle items, the "Clik!Case" plastic storage containers. This company never really developed, and I feel sure Tom knew this would be the case. I am confident this was his way of taking care of two long-term employees who were loyal and dedicated to the company. I will always be grateful to him for his kindness and desire to make sure my transition was without financial pressure. After a year of trying to restart this promotional business, we closed the company. Again, I had to find another job.

This is exactly what happened. I found jobs, and worked for other companies, but nothing came close to the fulfillment and pure joy I had felt while working with the best people in the best environment I had ever known. I found nothing close to the Outer Circle work experience for the rest of my career. This is not new, not rare, not the exception to people and their careers. This kind of thing happens every day, and we are all forced at various times to move on. I have handled this move poorly, and this failure is my responsibility. I broke my own rule of thinking how great things were at Outer Circle, and not embracing the change life sent my way. I have had more jobs than I like to think about since the Outer Circle days. One of the worst was my experience of investing in and eventually owning a restaurant. While the business was fun and an overall good social experience, it was not a great financial situation. Working eighty hours a week for about $1.00 per hour is not a great way to make your fortune. Still, I enjoyed most of my time at "Sid's" on 8th Street in Downtown Opelika. Other work included a regional manager position with a medical-safety company, a five-year stint with Allstate Insurance, General Manager training with Pilot/Flying J, and a few other dead-end positions.

In 2015, I moved to Flagler Beach, FL, for a new Allstate sales position. It was not a terrible business and one that can be very satisfying. When you sit down with someone who has suffered a tremendous loss and tell them they are fully protected, it is a great feeling. When you hand over a check to cover loss or damage from an accident, fire, or occasionally a death, you can see the relief people feel in knowing they made good choices.

Still, I did not feel fulfilled or completely satisfied. I kept thinking this was because of my not being completely happy with my career direction and my financial situation. I had built up a fair amount of debt, and my earnings were such it would take some time to get the debt paid off. I was no longer making substantial money and not able to buy most anything I wanted or travel whenever we felt like making a trip. I was, for the first time in my career, working hard to make ends meet. I was grinding through every week and working harder, for less than ever before. Just like millions of other hard-working people who accomplish this task every single day. I was still in a good place, surrounded by people who loved and cared about me. My wife Wendy and I developed a plan for me to move to Florida for a new job, rent a house or condo, and she would follow me within the next year.

What I didn't understand was the fact I was not happy with myself, and I was not really looking at who I was and how I was living my life. Very few people close to me would have noticed this change in my life, as I have always been a great actor. As I have said often about my life and sales career, I know how to play a role. As a salesperson, I would drive to the airport, fly to my destination, get the rental car and check into the hotel as me. I would plan my meeting, then drive to the customer's location. As I walked to the door of every business, I would start playing the role of Sid, the Sales Manager. I would stay in character for the meeting, for lunch after, or as long as necessary. Then as I walked away, returned to the airport or started my drive home, I would return to being just me, with all my insecurities, worries, impatience and daydreams about becoming content with my life.

This was how things moved ahead, even as I moved to Flagler Beach. I continued to be unhappy with my career direction and more concerned about my finances. I could not shake the feeling of being a failure, and those negative feelings flooded back into my thoughts constantly. I could not get myself into a content, non-stressed frame of mind. I really struggled to get through each day, but something unusual was about to happen and it would change my life.

For the first time I could remember, I said to myself, don't focus on the negatives and just get through today. In fact, I prayed a great deal about what step to take. My sweet Mother's insistence on dragging me to church every Sunday for sixteen years had instilled a sense of faith in me. I decided to do my best to be positive or at least neutral. If I could not be content, I promised myself I could at least not be miserable. The next day, my daughter Julie left me a voicemail. She told me a friend had mentioned me to her husband and let him know I was open to making a career change. The result was his company wanted to talk to me.

I was excited and hopeful, but again, I caught myself and decided to just be patient and not assume anything would work out. I spoke to the President of the company, one of three brothers running the business. We held a telephone interview and set up a meeting. By Friday of this same week, they offered me a sales job. I was their first and only outside business development salesperson. It would be impossible to explain the joy I felt about this opportunity. A tremendous sense of relief came over me. I vowed to make the best of this opportunity and work harder than I had ever worked before. I wanted to make this job my last before retiring, and finally return to being the happy, content person I had been during my Outer Circle days. Soon, my wife left her current job and moved to Florida. Suddenly, all the things making me so uncomfortable were changing and good things seemed to be falling into place.

It is important to know I was joining a business in which I had no experience. We were a CNC facility and made precision parts. I didn't even know what CNC stood for. I soon learned it meant Computer Numerical Control, the world of Haas Automation, Mazak and other CNC equipment makers. I did not care one bit about my inexperience within this business. I found my old confidence, but with a new drive and desire to be a success. At this point, it would seem to be a fairy tale ending to my search for meaningful work, peace of mind and all other good things. As we all know, life is filled with challenges and change. No, this was not the case at all.

In the first year of employment I studied, wrote hundreds of emails, sent LinkedIn In-mails, made hundreds of calls, managed my Sales-Force files accurately, and did my job well. I landed five major accounts for the business, which produced somewhere around $3.0 to $3.5 million in sales. The company paid me a small base salary plus commissions. In 2016, those sales paid off, and I returned to making a very good income and feeling important and vital to the health of the company. Because of the slowdown in the oil producing/refining industry, our company had lost about $3.0M in total sales from the previous year. My new customers not only kept us going, but slightly increased our overall sales totals. I was moving ahead with my growth and development with this company and making a real difference. A short time later, we sold our condo and bought a house nearby. We were in a good place, and life seemed to be very good.

So, everything sounds perfect here, and it sounded perfect for me until I realized this company had some major problems. The biggest issue was the owner of the company was an absolute nut job. He treated people with total disrespect and fired people for crazy random reasons. Even though I wanted this job to be as perfect as possible, I knew it was a terrible environment. Sexist, unprofessional and embarrassing behavior was the norm. I watched the owner walk through the building one Friday, beer in hand, celebrating his firing of multiple employees, and his own superior business intelligence. He seemed to believe he was the smartest business owner in the world. As he walked through the office, he called out people's name and in this very open forum, said, "Your pay is cut by $2.00 an hour. Be a team player and live with it". What a damned fool. The biggest narcissist I had ever known. I had returned to a business environment I despised and had worked to escape. Oh well, I thought, I am producing, so he isn't targeting me. This place would never be Outer Circle, and I needed to maintain my position and income. I could at least hope for a positive change at some point, so on I went. I kept selling, managing, and trying to increase our sales volume day by day.

When I would ask what we would do when we didn't have more manufacturing capacity, I was told we would buy more machines and expand. This sounded reasonable, so I kept my head down and kept selling. I found more and more success until one day I was told to stop looking for new customers. We could barely handle the business we had, so they directed me to do more program management and develop the business with existing customers. During my second year, I tried to slow down and understand exactly what was happening around me. I had the desire to change the lousy situations I saw people dealing with almost daily. The lies to customers and the disregard for contract requirements bothered me. But I can honestly say I was powerless to make any changes. I resigned myself to the fact this was another, not so great job, but one I had nurtured and developed into a reasonably well-paid position. I also resigned myself to surviving the conditions and working until retirement. I was more content, but still not truly happy.

On another early morning walk, I thought about what I was doing and what I felt. Clearly, I was not where I should be internally, and I still worried about things too much. Through this entire ordeal, and yes, it was an ordeal; I accepted the BS, the lies, and the mistreatment of employees and customers alike. I took my commission checks and believed things would get better. A few months later, I was elevated to the management team. I was one of three managers tasked with oversight of the business in our specific departments. We were told the company was for sale, and with this move, the crazy owner would take his money, go away, and we could move ahead as a real company. We would, at some point, soon become a professional organization and really grow.

Happily, I bought this idea and worked even harder. After working on one specific aerospace program for about eighteen months, we secured a four-year, $4.0 M contract for a component in the LEAP commercial jet engine. This was a significant moment for me. I had worked hard to keep this program alive and had done my best to land it. With the decision being made, I felt an even stronger sense of accomplishment despite all the frustrations and distractions. While this contract was exciting and very fulfilling to me, I wondered even more how we would meet this new business demand. How could we manage this new volume and maintain other contracts with our low headcount and unwillingness to support the business growth?

These issues should have caused me great concern, worry and more anxiety. Somehow, the exact opposite happened. I felt, maybe for the very first time at this place, my work truly mattered. I felt I was a success. I had gone into a strange business with no support or training and developed a successful sales strategy which produced much more than anyone had expected. For the first time in a very long time, I was at peace. I was content and comfortable with anything that might happen. It was one of the most empowering, uplifting feelings I had ever had. This mental change also freed me from the trap so many people deal with each day, a damn lousy work environment. Maybe it's an abusive boss or a toxic environment, but many people are stuck in these situations and work really means misery. I realized I had been fortunate enough to have avoided this situation most of my career and again I realized how lucky I had been. The lousy conditions were why I was so frustrated and angry. I focused on my newfound sense of calm and ignored the problems I could not impact at work.

Less than a month later, my boss told me money was tight, and he had to let me go. While I could have emptied my stored-up anger and frustration, I did the opposite. I acted professionally and calmly told him how I felt. I explained how much I felt I had contributed. How I had worked hard on every new task they assigned me as the company cut more and more staff to feed the owner's greed. Then I stood, shook his hand and said, "You have always been good to me and I wish you the best personally. Goodbye". I left feeling unsettled, not thrilled, but calm and at peace with myself. On my drive home, my cell rang and my former boss, the owner's brother, let me know he was sorry about the decision to let me go. He also told me he would pay my commissions for the next four months. At least my calm manner had created some goodwill with him. The fact he was a solid, standup guy helped this situation. Once again, life had thrown me a big curve ball. I was about to be sixty-two years old and unemployed. At this point, I was potentially too young to retire comfortably and maybe too old to be a viable new hire.

The huge lesson I learned was to do what I could and trust things would work out in the end. This most recent example of a difficult circumstance seemed to answer many of my questions. I learned and understood the outcome and the daily management of my life is my responsibility. Life and living are not about what good or bad things happen. It is not only about making lots of money, although having enough money to live your life is very important. The answers to so many questions that have caused me to always ask "what is my life all about" are simple. I have the absolute power to feel good or feel lost and anxious. I can't control other people or events. I can worry or choose to worry less or not at all. No other person has this power, only me. As I thought more and more about how I had handled every difficult position I faced, a very slow realization came to me. My life, like the lives of most people, is not orderly. It does not follow my plans or my dreams. It is filled with a constant series of challenges. Sometimes life gives us wonderful experiences, great relationships and at other times terrible situations and very poor relationships. Life sends us very good people and some not so good.

When I recall my friends along this journey, I can honestly say I do not deserve them. From my high school buddies to business/work friends, neighborhood friends and everyone in between, I am blessed to know them. I have friends I don't speak with for months, then we reconnect, and it is as if we were together the day before. These people have loved me, helped me, admonished me, challenged and advised me, but most of all, they have cared about me. If you have those relationships, you have a great gift. Cherish them and never doubt how important they all are to you.

What I slowly understood and realized was my responsibility to myself and the people I cared about. I have the ability to make good and solid choices, even when things around me are not going very well. Will I ever be totally happy, probably not, but I can be as happy as I allow and drive myself to be. I can stop worrying about what anyone else thinks about me and my life situation. Have I been so prideful, so ignorant to think my tough times were worse than those others have experienced? Did I really feel I deserved to be insulated and protected against all uncomfortable or unpleasant things I faced? The answer is clearly no, not at all. My life is really about how I handle the good and bad things I face every single day. I am confident the positive impact of my time at Outer Circle helped me reach this healthier place in my life. I left that place with skills and confidence I never had before.

I dissected the many good and bad events from my career, then tried to imagine what might have happened with a different reaction or point of view. I finally saw how the less than wonderful experiences were not as common as the good experiences. I realized those bad times fed into a weak portion of my personality. My long-established trait of feeling anxiety and fear was something I had allowed to develop. This feeling was supported by my wanting all things to be orderly and happy in my life and with the people around me. As I understood these things, I felt foolish. The answers I found had once seemed unattainable, yet they were very simple, and my new clarity about life was something most people seemed to fully understand. It is as if all the things those older, wiser people had said to me were actually the keys to a happier life. All the people I used to ignore as unrealistic when they told me to be happier, and not worry about things you can't control, were right. To everyone who told me to work hard, develop patience and do everything the best I could, let me say you were 100% correct.

About this time, I began writing my first book, "A Backwards Glance", which was a collection of life events and stories from business and personal relationships I felt were unusual and interesting. This led me to write a chapter about Outer Circle

Products and this process took me back to this great experience and our beautiful, principled culture. This exercise helped me enjoy writing more than I could have expected. About half way through writing the book, I was offered a new job. I was hired as the Director of Business Development for a nearby non-profit organization. While I had no experience with fundraising in the non-profit sector, I could write, communicate well, and I was an organized manager. I accepted the position and began my initial non-profit work.

They charged me with raising money and increasing our meager donor base. It was hard work since there was no training and the previous development manager had left the company abruptly. We were raising money for the visually impaired and our main fund-raising activities were large dinner events called, "Dining in the dark". We seated diners in a pitch-dark dining room and had them eat their meal while effectively being blind. We also had one of our blind clients sit at each table to help them manage their meals. We sold individual tickets, eight person tables, and sponsorships for this 250-person dinner. These dinners were well received and memorable experiences for everyone involved. They were a nightmare to plan, coordinate, and manage. However, we raised thousands of dollars with these events, and this was the primary goal. In the real world, money drives the programs and training needed by non-profits. The life changes and improvements from our training are the important payoff, but donations and fund-raising events created these opportunities. We also had an incredibly dedicated and effective team of employees who were totally supportive of my work. Our staff worked hard, committed to the after-hours time to make our events successful, and helped make our clients' lives better.

The only problem we had in the company was our paranoid and often absent CEO. This individual disappeared for weeks on end when we were doing the very difficult work for our fund-raising events. In my two years with the company, she was away from the office at least fifty percent of the time. I do not know how a company president could take so much vacation time. It was an odd work experience since the internal environment was completely different depending on her presence. If she was away, our office was respectful, efficient and relaxed. Her presence in the office hurt morale, created busy work and led to a toxic work environment. I hated to hear about conversations where our staff was threatened with the loss of their jobs. This was a sad thing to experience with employees who worked very hard with little to no direction. These folks made very little money and had limited career opportunities. Many people on our staff were managing some type of visual impairment or other health challenges.

It took me a while to understand what was going on in our office as I was in and out most days. Since I was new, the team didn't immediately feel comfortable letting me know what was going on. This job was like working for two totally different companies. The only similarity was the constant hard work and dedication of our team. After a few months, I realized my boss was disorganized, abrasive and disliked by many people inside and outside our office. Even with seeing her personality first hand, I was surprised at the anger she generated. Looking back, the situation is much clearer. I was taking work off her hands and solving problems without asking for help. I was not a great talent, but I was experienced enough to figure things out and independent enough to make important decisions on my own. I simply made her work life easier, so I was left alone.

I had never written a newsletter or coordinated monthly luncheons with guest speakers prior to this job. Our office manager, Tricia, took the time to help, and walked me through the steps needed for both tasks. She was a great resource and highly regarded by everyone in the company. Actually, everyone valued her input except our CEO. She resented the respect Tricia was shown and also resented how most everyone enjoyed being around her. People were drawn to her knowledge and positive approach, so this naturally represented a threat to the boss. The decision to let her go had a terrible impact on our staff and I became convinced it was not the place for me. I stayed on until the next scheduled fund-raising dinner was completed.

My last official act was to complete an exit interview in writing. My letter was honest and direct. I passed on the detailed notes on the erratic behavior of our CEO. The board chairman contacted me and expressed shock and concern over the details in my letter. Still, this conversation was also BS as no changes were ever made at the agency. It remained a toxic, unfair and manipulative environment. Like most of these situations, weak leadership and an apathetic board did not generate any changes.

This situation was not unheard of or an exception to a great many business segments or company environments. The worst thing about a toxic workplace is the pressure, stress and anxiety it places on people who are in a weak position to fight back. Bullying managers might not kill a company, but they absolutely create needless turnover, stymie productivity, and limit personal growth. These are the individuals who should be eliminated from the workplace or, at the least, removed from a position of influence, evaluation, or control.

While I was working on this book, I noticed some common traits shared by poor managers and leaders. The biggest failing trait is fear. The fear of sharing power, trusting their team, and the overall fear of somehow being diminished by others' success are dangerous. This fear fuels erratic and misdirected emotions, judgement and criticism.

Another terrible trait of bullying and awful managers is arrogance disguised as leadership and decision making. When someone in a power position decides they alone have the skills, intelligence and business acumen to set the proper course for a business, the flow of shared ideas declines or stops. This kills the desire most employees have to help their company become more successful. It drains the emotional commitment needed to think, take chances, and offer ideas. If a company culture allows anyone to have a separate set of rules or standards, your culture becomes divided. This mistake labels people as having or not having power or influence. Nothing is more demotivating than knowing your input is not heard or even wanted. These conditions turn potentially developmental employees into clock watchers, who are waiting for the acceptable time to leave.

Over the course of my years as a salesperson and sales manager, I have seen several very good company environments and a few horrible environments. I feel very fortunate to have worked in at least one principled business culture offering a powerful and freeing environment. I am sure of one thing, slogans, well-meaning themes and empty words do not make any work environment better. These things are shallow, temporary, band-aid steps instead of meaningful changes. There are many books, workshops, courses and lectures on improving and protecting company environments. Many are attempting to add a positive idea or action, but most do not create actual change. Before you think about impacting your culture, it would be best to examine it in depth and be honest about what you find. Perhaps the best idea for decision makers would be to change or re-create your culture to offer the best work environment possible. This step requires leadership from the top and a consistent commitment from the most powerful voices in a company. It also requires a single set of rules or guidelines on behaviors for everyone. There can be no exemptions to the rules, no kingdoms, no functional silos and no prima donnas.

A principled business culture isn't some type of progressive or socialist doctrine. It comes from empowering everyone to have an equal voice in the setting of common guidelines and rules of interaction. This voice must be open to speaking what you truly feel as long as it is respectful and given as your honest feedback. This also means everyone must understand there is a requirement of sound business practices in the daily work. These practices are directed by managers who must lead with the same rules of respect and clarity. It must be understood that managers must give direction and, when given respectfully, that direction must be followed. This culture is not a "do as you like" way of behavior, but a partnership in taking measured risks, being responsible for your actions and accomplishing great results. The steps are very clear and easy to say, but incredibly hard to execute. A principled business culture is very much like a living thing. It must have attention, care and dedicated action by everyone who works within it.

Even if you are not in a company with anything like the Outer Circle principled business culture, you can make important changes to your behavior. You can create your own list of principles with an examination of yourself and the environment of your workplace. I would pursue this review by making a detailed set of notes. Write your initial feelings on:

-ownership
-managers
-all departments
-fellow employees
-advancement opportunities
-the company's support of its customers, vendors and community
-compensation
-is your voice heard when you make suggestions or give opinions

When you complete this step, go back and look at your notes and again examine your evaluations. Do this before you complete a critical self-evaluation, since this step is the one you have direct control over. If you notice any incidence or acceptance of disrespect, spend more time evaluating that area. Examine it as thoroughly as you can. Peel back every layer and identify why and how it happens as best you can. The presence of disrespect directly contradicts the idea and existence of an inclusive, positive culture. Give your workplace environment a name or a ranking as it stands today. Do this to establish a baseline.

As you review your list, make a critical evaluation of every manager, the department they manage, and the people in those departments. You can rank them or grade them if this helps you get a clear picture.

Look at advancement opportunities for yourself and anyone else you have insight on. Determine if any advancement trends seem out of balance or in conflict with ability. Do you see favoritism or any subtle discriminatory practices?

Everyone should be able to make an honest judgement on how the company treats its own employees, customers, vendors, or clients. Is the company focused on making demands or is it open to partnerships with these vital areas? Does your company have any policies or common practices giving back to your community?

While the direct knowledge of other employees' compensation is usually limited, if not missing, you can evaluate your own benefits and compensation in detail. Do you feel properly compensated for the work you do, or is something missing?

Evaluate every method you and others have to give an opinion, make a complaint or ask for more information. Since the most common spot for these items is usually the human resources manager or department, you should review your relationships there and rate its accessibility and responsiveness. Do you have an open flow of communication with your direct manager? Can you add your opinion or concerns? What is your relationship with that manager and what impacts it most?

When you begin your personal review, it is important to be honest and without self-serving bias. Most of us find this step difficult since it is tough to evaluate our own behavior and actions critically. Attempt to critique your own words, actions, and motives as deeply as you can. If you are a manager or supervisor with authority over others, give your style a thorough review and critical evaluation. Your ability to be self-aware and a critical review of your influence can provide valuable insight.

After you have completed these difficult and time-consuming steps, you are better able to determine how your actions fit with the description you gave the other areas you investigated. The last question in your self-evaluation should be, "Are you a positive, neutral or negative influencer?" Where would the people you impact rank your style? Even if you have no responsibility for another employee, your influence and impact are important. Everyone's actions have a direct impact on your company's culture and the workplace environment.

Finally, what do you do with the information from your overall and personal review? The first thing you can do is determine if you can make any beneficial changes to your company environment. Most people will find limited opportunities to make major changes. However, everyone can change their own behavior. You can create your own principled culture of one. You can use the principles I offer or make a new list. With respect for everyone as the first rule, you can interact and perform better. Your changes might have a critical and important impact on everyone around you, but more importantly, they will make you better. If you are a department manager or a team leader, you can pass on many of these guidelines and behaviors to your teams. If you are an equity owner, or a person of authority and influence, you can implement your own principled culture or focus on making your company environment better.

I would agree with some critics of this philosophy that it works best in a small to medium company. Without doubt, company size impacts the ability to monitor and support a major cultural change. However, company size does not disqualify this cultural change. It may take longer and it may be much more difficult, but positive changes can be made. Empowering, trusting and respecting your employees is a beneficial and powerful tool for any business.

I hope this collection of ideas, examples, and personal experiences can be helpful to everyone who reads this book. I will always believe the principled company culture we created at Outer Circle Products was the best example of a positive work experience. I hope to develop some additional tools and instruction on this process for anyone with interest. I am always open to respectful conversations and opinions on my social media outlets as well. Finally, I sincerely wish every business and individual employee the best success with their careers and personal goals.

About the Author

Sid Mickle was born a Southerner with a lifelong passion for storytelling. A native of Lafayette, Alabama, he crisscrossed the country for forty years during his sales management career before returning to East Alabama. Finally, back at home, he pursues his passion for writing, gardening and restoring classic vehicles. He also finds time to follow his beloved Cincinnati Red's baseball club.

After taking years to write his first book, "A Backwards Glance", book two, "Who Killed Glenna"? was published six months later. This book is the first of a three-part series on the life of the main character Sam Bennett. The second book in the series, "A Few Bad Men" is expected to be published in early 2022.

This book, Sid's third, "Principles, How to Create A Principled Business Culture", is available on Amazon in e-book and paperback versions. Two additional books, "If I Could Turn Back Time" and "Another Backwards Glance", are planned for publication in mid to late 2022.

All published works by Sid Mickle can also be found at:

www.sidmicklepublications.com

Personalized books can be ordered here as well. Specific messages can usually be accommodated with a reasonable time allowance.

You can also follow his writing career, read excerpts from new books and communicate with him on his Facebook page, Sid Mickle Publications. We are happy to answer questions about characters, current books, future projects and general questions on most any writing topic. If you have questions about writing a book of your own, please reach out at any time.

A personal request from the author:

If you are comfortable with the idea, please leave your review on Amazon. You can go to Amazon.com, locate this book by simply entering the title, and find the review section. If you are willing, please leave a review on the book page. Book reviews are the most valuable thing an author can receive from readers. Positive reviews encourage others to buy the book, since they are a confirmation of its value to them.

If you are compelled to add a review, please know each one is invaluable to most authors, but especially to new authors searching for a following. Also, know every review is very much appreciated.

Acknowledgements

The following information represents and acknowledges many of the people I worked with during my nearly forty-year business career. These are the people who were influential, positive and often very supportive of me during my time there. This list will not be absolutely complete, as I simply cannot recall every name. For that, I apologize and ask for understanding from anyone I missed.

McNeil Consumer Products Company

Mario, Larry, Bill, Dave, Bruce, Marie, Donna, Cindy, Karen, June, Willard, Marty, Kim, Stacy, Jim F, Jim H, Mary, Gary, Mike, Tom, Rick, Joe, Skip, Rich, Jerry, Sonny, Harold, Glenna, Shannon, Tony, Chris, Mark, Debbie, John, Terri, and last, but certainly not least, Paul.

Ragu Foods Division of Unilever

Lee, Stan, Hank, Cheryl, John, Ed, Larry, Paul, Chris, and Mike

Outer Circle Products, LTD.

Rod, Rick, Marty, Andy, Rob, Stewart, Bert, Susan, Jennifer, LeAnn, Anne, Karen, Katrina, Nikki, Robin, Rose, Jodi, Carol, Sue, Kent (aka Keith Comstock), Patricia, Henry, Maurice, Mary, Larry, Tom, Charlie, Stacey, Mike, Don, Sean, Rick, Kim, Margaret, Maureen and Mel.

In-Zone Brands

Jake, Chris, Andrew, Bobby, Nikole, Marie, Nicole, Mindy, Gunner, Ed, Karen, Frenchy, Jen, Jessica, Dana, and Bert, (again)

Additionally, I want to acknowledge the biggest supporters of my efforts to write each of the books in my catalog.

Wendy, Collin, Julie, Audrey, Randy, Neal, Lamar, Richard, Susan, Cathy, Becky, Angela, Harold, Bob, Becky, Cindy, Paul, Christine & Christine, Mario, Larry, Gary, Lane, Eddie, Calvin, David, Dave, Brandi, Brooke, Jeff, June, Patricia, Alisa, Donnie, Titus, Zach, Chris, Christy, my dear friend, Wayne, and many others who have called or written with words of support.

Your kindness, information, encouragement and patience are invaluable to my limited success in writing good material. I love you all for your help and support, more than you know.

There are many teachers and administrators who were influential and powerful supporters. Here are a few I remember well;

Ms. Cox, Mr. East, Ms. Burton, Ms. Leverette-Jones, Ms. Anthony, Ms. Thomas, Ms. Andrews, Mr. Green, Ms. Higgins, Ms., Prather, MS, Hood, Ms. Graves, Ms. Walker, Professor Creek and Professor Garrett, Professor Rabinowitz

I want to acknowledge and thank a few special coaches and one martial arts instructor I had the absolute pleasure of working with during my young life as an athlete and later on. These fine men had and still have a tremendous influence on me. I owe you all so much, and I love you all for your time, lessons, patience and dedication to teach and train your students and athletes.

Coach Pugh, Coach Nettles, Coach Howard, Coach Lindsey, Coach Lee, Coach Phillips, Coach Jones, Coach Allen and Master Johnson

I also want to thank my sister-in-law, Christine for her incredible contributions to the editing of this book. She always speaks her mind and challenges me on any point she feels needs clarity. Thank you so much, you are a great talent.

Finally, I want to thank and acknowledge the class of 1973, who are my incredible friends and classmates. I also note my appreciation for every member of our sports teams from Fall, 1970 through Spring, 1973, and especially my senior teammates from our 1972/73 teams;

Gary, Fred, Richard, Tommy, Ronnie, Randy, Neal

Some of my dear friends and teammates are no longer with us and we all miss them terribly. Each of these wonderful friends are always on my side and supporting my meager writing efforts.

www.ingramcontent.com/pod-product-compliance
Lightning Source LLC
Chambersburg PA
CBHW052313220526
45472CB00001B/98